Producing Opera for America

Producing Opera for America

by Herbert Graf

Atlantis Books Zürich / New York

TO MARY CURTIS ZIMBALIST

Acknowledgements

The *research* for this study was done under a grant from the Rockefeller Foundation.

Its *publication* was made possible by Mrs. Efrem Zimbalist, President of the Curtis Institute of Music in Philadelphia.

The *material* I owe to many friends and institutions both in America and Europe. Of these, I wish to express my special thanks to the Metropolitan Opera Guild for statistics; the Central Opera Service for efficient handling of questionnaires sent to community and school opera groups; *Musical America;* the offices of ANTA (American National Theatre and Academy); The Lincoln Center for the Performing Arts; the *Bühnentechnische Rundschau,* Prof. Walther Unruh, Editor, and various architects for illustrations; and to Marjorie Mansouri and Max Röthlisberger for assistance on manuscript and sketches.

And last, but most important, I am especially grateful to Floris Ferwerda for his constant and decisive help in preparing and editing the manuscript; and to Dr. Martin Hürlimann, Director of Atlantis-Verlag, for his personal interest in its publication.

Contents

Introduction. The Aim

American talent in Europe
In the spring of 1955, as I was about to leave for my work at European summer festivals, I received a call from David Wodlinger, Director of the Institute of International Education administering the Fulbright Program. Mr. Wodlinger asked me to contact American musicians studying in Italy and Austria. It was an assignment I undertook with great interest. In Europe, as in America, I was impressed by the unusual amount of talent I found among the young American singers, composers and conductors. But I was distressed by the one plea all of them made: "Please help us find a place in a European opera house! We don't want to go home because we can't find an opportunity to work and earn a living there in our own field."

Lack of professional opera companies in America
On my return to New York I discussed with Mr. Wodlinger a problem which seems to me most urgent: namely, *the need to establish more professional opera companies in the United States.* I outlined some ideas I had on this subject, and he introduced me to the Directors of the Humanities Division of the Rockefeller Foundation. I pointed out to them that it appeared useless and contradictory to give scholarships to young operatic artists unless at the same time we create new possibilities for their professional activity in America.

In recent years the American public has become increasingly interested in good music, particularly opera. This has led to the creation of great numbers of symphony orchestras, music schools and opera workshops. The time has now come to take a further and more difficult step: professional opera companies must be established throughout the United States, so organized that they can operate on a secure artistic and financial basis.

After twenty-five years of experience in America, working in every branch of the operatic field, I no longer dream of grand subsidies for American opera, similar to the $3,600,000 grant that my native Vienna still pays every year to support its two opera houses. I say this without bitterness, because after studying the historical and sociological background of opera in both Europe and America,* I fully realize that the European tradition cannot serve as a basis for the organization of opera in the United States. The origins and growth of American opera have followed entirely different patterns. America must chart her own course.

Indigenous forces

On the other hand, my survey of the indigenous forces now at work in American opera revealed enormous potentialities in this field.** Elementary and even amateurish though these forces may be, in many cases, at this moment they present completely new possibilities which clearly foreshadow the American opera of tomorrow.

Those who have attended the conferences of the Central Opera Service*** in New York can appreciate how rapidly interest in opera has grown. Valiant attempts are being made throughout the country to organize community opera, to produce opera on television, and particularly to develop opera on the educational and workshop level.

Problems of American opera production

These conferences have made it evident, however, that nearly all professional opera companies lack the financial security necessary for a healthy artistic and economic existence. One is also struck with the vast disagreement and general confusion about operatic terminology and standards, the problem of whether to present traditional or "modernized" productions, the question of singing foreign operas in English, the overlap between professional and educational institutions and activities, the problem of collaboration between operatic and symphonic organizations, the philosophy and economics of sponsorship, the problem of procuring existing theatres and stage equipment, and the design characteristics desirable in the theatres of tomorrow.

The need for a comprehensive study of the entire field is clear. We must first discover the operatic facts of life as they exist in America today, and then discuss how we can create the American opera of tomorrow.

For the first time in history, the Lincoln Center for the Performing Arts in New

---

* Herbert Graf, *The Opera and its Future in America* (New York: W. W. Norton & Co., 1941).
** Idem., *Opera for the People* (Minneapolis: University of Minnesota Press, 1951).
*** The Central Opera Service is an advisory agency sponsored by the National Council of the Metropolitan Opera Association. It serves operatic groups throughout the United States.

York will bring together professional organizations in the fields of opera, symphony, dance, drama and education. In this unique project opera will have an active relationship with the other arts. The grand concept of Lincoln Center points up the basic question: What is the place of opera in the cultural life of the American community today, and by what methods can opera in America achieve artistic and economic support?

The European background In seeking answers to these questions, it is natural to turn first to Europe, where opera originated, and where a solidly established system of operation has developed over the centuries. Let us see how opera is functioning there. But let us make our trip accompanied by two stalwart companions, history and common sense. They will help us understand the reasons for many puzzling phenomena in the strange world of opera, where high *C*'s so often drown out the voice of reason. With this European background we can then study the actual facts of the operatic situation in America. Thus equipped, we will be in a position to make concrete proposals for practical steps by which opera can be established as an integral cultural activity in the United States.

Part I. Opera in Europe

1. SPONSORSHIP

Government subsidy

An American visiting Europe is impressed immediately by the great number of opera theatres. These for the most part operate on a secure, long-term financial basis, particularly in the German-speaking middle-European countries, thanks to national, state or municipal government support.

Germany

The government subsidies of today continue a long tradition that began when emperors and dukes chose to exhibit their wealth by sponsoring splendid opera productions. Prior to 1914, Germany had twenty-five principalities, which owned and sponsored about fifty theatres. During the Nineteenth and Twentieth Centuries these theatres were taken over by democratic governments, but the tradition of government subsidy was continued. Today in the Ruhr district and its immediate neighborhood alone, fourteen cities have subsidized opera companies. Some of these theatres are not more than a half-hour distant from each other, yet most of them operate ten and one-half months during the year.

Germany now has a total of 130 subsidized theatres. Of these, eight present opera exclusively, and fifty-two produce operetta and plays in addition to opera. Eighteen are state theatres, supported by the state and the provinces; ninety-six are municipal theatres, supported essentially by cities. Sixteen are *Landesbühnen,* or "theatres of the country," most of which tour within their region. In addition there are twenty-five commercial theatres. In all, the German theatres employ a total of 16,030 artists and technicians on a regular basis.

Typical subsidies include approximately $1,750,000 (DM 7.000.000) for the West Berlin Opera House, $1,675,000 (DM 6.700.000) for the Hamburg Opera House,* $2,193,100 (DM 9,100.000) for Cologne's new theatre (opera and drama), $850,000 (DM 3.400.000) for the two theatres at Mannheim, and $700,000

(DM 2.800.000) for the municipal theatres at Gelsenkirchen. If we break these figures down on a per capita basis, we find that each citizen of West Berlin contributes $1.29 (DM 5.16) per year; each citizen of Hamburg, 96 cents (DM 3.85) per year; Mannheim, $2.74 (DM 10.95); and Gelsenkirchen, $2.04 (DM 8.14).**

Government subsidies granted to the German theatres each year total between $35,000,000 and $37,500,000 (DM 140.000.000 to 150.000.000).

During the 1954–55 season, 5,390,250 people attended opera performances in Germany. The attendance at *all* German theatre performances, including opera, breaks down as follows: 27 per cent held subscription tickets; 10.5 per cent belonged to youth and student groups; 29.6 per cent bought tickets at the box office; 4.1 per cent were supplied free tickets as employees; and 28.8 per cent were members of *Besuchergemeinden* (Organizations of Visitors), which subscribe to performances en bloc at reduced rates.***

Opera is equally well established in Austria, Switzerland and Italy, and to a somewhat lesser extent in Sweden, France and England. Everywhere it is subsidized. To an American, these subsidies often seem quite fabulous.

Austria

Vienna, for example, is today the capital of a country containing only six and one-half million people—considerably less than the population of New York City. Yet Vienna supports two opera houses that operate all year, plus a third operatic activity in the historic Redoutensaal. Emulating the generosity of

---

* The Hamburg Opera's budget is based on the assumption that 66.6 per cent of its expenses will be taken in at the box office. There are about 14,000 subscribers. Cologne has fourteen subscription series: one series of nine premières, and thirteen series which include nine operas and three plays each. For these performances one-half the house is held open for public ticket sale. Mondays and Tuesdays are *Volksbühne* (Socialist Party) and *Theatergemeinde* (Catholic Party) performances at reduced prices.

** The average annual per capita tax in West Germany for theatre support alone comes to $1.43 (DM 6.—), according to the detailed statistics in the study by the architect Werner Kallmorgen, *Was heisst und zu welchem Ende baut man Kommunaltheater?* (Darmstadt: Verlag Das Beispiel, 1955).

*** These figures on German theatres have been compiled from three sources: (*a*) The detailed reports published by the Office of Statistics and Elections of the City of Braunschweig, covering the season 1954–55 and extended to 1956; (*b*) a study of the German theatre made by the magazine *Rendez-vous des théâtres du Monde* (Paris, December 15, 1957); and (*c*) the official publication *Deutscher Bühnenalmanach* (Hamburg: Genossenschaft Deutscher Bühnen-Angehörigen, 1958, 1959, 1960).

Emperor Franz Joseph I, who once ruled an empire of 52,000,000 people, the present State of Austria paid a subsidy of approximately $4,840,000 (121.000.000 Schillings) during 1960 for the federal theatres in Vienna: the Vienna State Opera, the Vienna Volksoper, and the Burgtheater (drama). Austria has still other opera companies performing in four other cities, in addition to the government-supported International Summer Festival at Salzburg, which receives another $800,000 (20.000.000 Schillings).

Switzerland

In Switzerland the only theater that presents opera exclusively is the Stadttheater at Zurich; but opera is also performed at the municipal theatres of Basle, Berne, Lucerne, Biel-Solothurn and St. Gallen. These theatres are supported by the individual cities, with some assistance from the cantons, or states, of the Swiss Confederation in which the cities are located, but *not* by the federal government.

Take Zurich, for example. Its Stadttheater is, as has been noted, Switzerland's only stage performing opera and operetta exclusively. During the 1958–59 season the theatre operated on a basis of 38.5 per cent income from the box office and 61.5 per cent subsidy from the City and Canton of Zurich. This subsidy amounted to about $800,000 (3.450.000 Swiss Francs). Among the various types of subscription series at reduced prices are thirty-six "Folk" performances. For these performances two-thirds of the regular ticket price is underwritten by the City as part of its subsidy. A similar allotment is granted for student performances. Other performances are sold en bloc to business organizations. In general, only the performances on Saturdays and Sundays are entirely available for public sale; on the other days (except Monday, when the theatre is closed) the attendance is partly or wholly guaranteed by various kinds of subscription or school performances. Prices range from 70 cents to $3.45 (3 to 15 Francs). An orchestra of 120 musicians presents symphony concerts as well as serving the opera. All personnel is engaged for the entire year, with a six-week paid vacation. The regular season runs from the beginning of September to the end of June; during June an International Festival is presented. Rehearsals for the new season begin about the middle of August, a minimum of three weeks prior to the opening. The Zurich Stadttheater mounts sixteen new productions each year: usually ten operas, four operettas, one evening of ballet and one Christmas production for children.

14

In Basle, where drama joins opera and operetta in the same theatre, the situation is in most respects similar. This house also runs on a year-round basis and receives its subsidy from the City and Canton of Basle. The federal government does not provide any additional assistance.

Italy

Now let us examine the situation in Italy. Although the Cabinet Zoli made radical reductions in opera subsidies during 1957, government interest was still evident. For example, La Scala at Milan received a grant of approximately $1,040,000 (L. 650.000.000); the Teatro dell'Opera in Rome, $1,016,000 (L. 635.000.000); the Teatro Comunale, Florence, some $664,000 (L. 415.000.000); San Carlo, in Naples, $640,000 (L. 400.000.000); the Teatro Massimo, Palermo, $214,400 (L. 134.000.000); La Fenice, in Venice, $196,800 (L. 123.000.000); Carlo Felice, Genova, $153,600 (L. 96.000.000); and Torino, $120,000 (L. 75.000.000). By 1960 the subsidies had again risen, to $1,440,000 (L. 900.000.000) for La Scala, and $800,000 (L. 500.000.000) for Florence, to name only two examples.

Nor is this all. In Italy the official state subsidies are augmented somewhat by sums received from city governments and from local institutions. These funds vary, from about $80,000 (L. 50.000.000) for La Scala and the Rome Opera, to some $48,000 (L. 30.000.000) for Naples' San Carlo. Moreover, the other Italian companies, including the outdoor summer opera at Verona, receive substantial government support.

Sweden

While theatres in Sweden are sponsored by the state and by municipalities, money for the state subsidy is procured in a somewhat novel way: It is raised through government-sponsored lotteries. Subsidies are distributed by the government on advice from the Theater Council. Of the eight permanent theatres in Sweden only the Royal Opera in Stockholm is devoted entirely to opera and ballet; opera alternates with light opera and drama at the Göteborg Lyric Theater and the Malmö Municipal Theater.

During the 1954–55 season the Opera at Stockholm received a state subsidy of $628,000 (3.140.000 Kronor). The Göteborg Lyric Theater and the Malmö Municipal Theater were given about $150,000 (750.000 Kronor) each. These state subsidies are augmented by grants from the cities. The Royal Opera in Stockholm received about $60,000 (300.000 Kronor) from the City of Stockholm, and about $20,000 (100.000 Kronor) from the Swedish Radio. In addition, it has available the interest from the so-called Reserve Fund of the Opera, which amounts to some $800,000 (4.000.000 Kronor).

At the same time, the Göteborg Lyric Theater had a grant of about $20,000 (100.000 Kronor) from the municipal government, and Malmö received an additional $31,000 (155.000 Kronor) from its city. These theatres pay no rent, and the Royal Opera, as well as the Göteborg Lyric Theater, are tax-exempt. Training schools attached to several of the theatres receive state and municipal grants. In addition to the permanent theatres, there are three state-supported touring theatres which travel throughout the country during the winter season. In all, grants by the Swedish government for theatre purposes in 1954–55 amounted to nearly $2,000,000 (10.000.000 Kronor).*

France

The French also support opera on a large scale. In 1955–56, the budget of the Paris Opéra and the Opéra-Comique ran to approximately $5,715,000 (NF 20.000.000). A National Commission which controls subsidy-supported theatres made available some $4,143,000 (NF 14.500.000). Only $1,314,000 (NF 4.600.000) was taken in at the box office, although an average of 1,500 spectators attended the Opéra each day (the seating capacity is 2,100); and about 800 people attended the Opéra-Comique (which seats 1,700). Outside Paris, opera was produced during 1955–56 in nine French cities—Strasbourg, Bordeaux, Lyon, Marseilles, Metz, Toulouse, Nancy, Mulhouse and Rouen. A subsidy of approximately $600,000 (NF 2.100.000) was granted for that purpose.**

England

In England, government assistance to the performing arts is relatively recent, but since 1945 the Arts Council of Great Britain has given much-needed support to opera, among the other arts. During the 1956–57 season the Covent Garden Opera House received the equivalent of $750,000, and Sadler's Wells received $350,000. Smaller grants were made to the Intimate Opera Society, the English

---

* These figures on the Swedish theatre are taken from an article by G. Z. Topelius, entitled, "What the Swedish State allows the Theatres," which appeared in *Theatre in Sweden*, a special issue of *World Theatre*, published by the International Theatre Institute with the assistance of UNESCO at Brussels (Elsevier, Vol. IV/2).

** Figures on French subsidies were taken from an article on this subject published in *Arts Spectacles*, issue of February 12, 1958, brought to my attention by Edouard Morot-Sir, Cultural Counselor of the French Embassy in New York and representative in the United States of French universities.

16

Opera Group and the Carl Rosa Touring Company, as well as to the Welsh National Opera Company and Glasgow Grand Opera Society.* In 1958–59, Covent Garden was given $1,013,000 (£362,000), and in 1959 the Arts Council allowed for the next three years a grant of 43 per cent of the approved expenditure, but with a maximum of $1,400,000 (£500,000) yearly. The funds are provided to the managements with the clear understanding that there will be no government interference in operating policy.

Canada It is interesting to note that on March 12, 1957, the Canadian Parliament followed Britain's lead by establishing the Canada Council, "which is charged with encouraging the arts, humanities and social sciences in Canada." The Canadian approach differs from the British inasmuch as the subsidy depends not on an annual Exchequer grant, but rather on an endowment fund of $50,000,000 for the arts. This endowment fund is matched by a fund of the same amount for capital expenditures on universities. The principle of government support of the arts, including opera, has been firmly established in our neighboring country to the north.

Although in Germany, Austria, Switzerland and Italy the annual subsidy normally covers only 40 to 50 per cent of expenses, in a number of instances the subsidy has been considerably greater. Italian subsidies for opera have at times run as high as 70 per cent of the total operating budget.

It is obvious from this brief survey that opera in Europe depends on a tradition of government subsidy and could hardly exist in its present form without it.

* See *Art in the Red, the Twelfth Annual Report of the Arts Council of Great Britain, 1956–57* (London: The Arts Council of Great Britain, 4 St. James Square, S.W.1).

2. THE OPERA THEATRE

The tradition of government sponsorship is clearly reflected in the design of European opera houses. If we look at these buildings in the light of their social history and practical function, we can easily see why auditorium and stage were designed as they were. They answer the social and aesthetic requirements of the audience they served, and the technical requirements of the performances originally staged. If we study these theatres in relation to present-day social and artistic requirements, however, we soon realize that the old baroque designs, fine as they were for their own times, are in many ways inadequate for ours.

Let us examine, briefly, the background of theatre design and see how the opera theatre has developed throughout the centuries.

Any theatre, of course, necessarily consists of two elements: an area for the audience and an area for the performers. The design of these elements should reflect the social relationships of the spectators and the technical requirements of the production.

Early theatres

Our Western heritage in the theatre goes back to Greece. When we visit a Greek theatre, such as that at Epidauros, we are overwhelmed by the perfection of its design in relation to the requirements. Here a democratic audience was to view a production in which the singing and dancing chorus was the chief element. The amphitheatre has excellent sightlines and acoustics, considering its size—an auditorium 387 feet in diameter, holding 16,000 people. The audience is grouped around the orchestra and stage, so that audience and actors are brought together in one community experience. The *skene* serves to indicate scenic background. Today our technical requirements are obviously more complicated, but in basic design this theatre—now 2,500 years old—is closer to the ideal than the majority of the theatres that followed it.

The next historic theatre form, the Roman theatre, I came to know by personal experience when I staged Handel's opera *Giulio Cesare*, with Renata Tebaldi and Cesare Siepi, at the Teatro Grande of Pompeii in 1950. The ancient theatre and stage were used without any alterations for this production, and I was again amazed at how perfect a solution to the problems of sight and sound had been found in this theatre, which seats 5,000. But here the sense of participation, felt so strongly at the Greek theatre of Epidauros, had been weakened somewhat by the Roman emphasis on the stage, with the "orchestra" reduced in size and dramatic function.

Condensing 1,500 years of history into a one-day trip, we go now to three theatres in northern Italy, all built within a span of less than forty years: the Palladio theatre at Vicenza (1585), the theatre by Scamozzi at Sabbioneta (1590), and the Teatro Farnese at Parma, designed by Aleotti (1619). This last is now being reconstructed in its original form after having suffered very heavy damage from bombardments during the war. These three theatres, built just at the time when opera was first developing, show us with dramatic clarity the process through which our opera stage evolved.

Italian Renaissance architects, who had studied the Roman theatre in the work, *On Architecture*, by Vitruvius,* revived the old design but added one new feature. They cut arches in the richly decorated wall of the Roman stage—first three arches (Vicenza, Sabbioneta), and then one big arch (Teatro Farnese). Into the openings they placed pictures painted with the new technique of Renaissance perspective. At first the picture had the nature of a permanent set, solidly constructed (Vicenza, Sabbioneta). Later it became flexible through the addition of wings, an invention of Aleotti, architect of the Teatro Farnese. The Teatro Farnese firmly established the use of the operatic "proscenium," and scenery painted in perspective.

The proscenium

This peep-hole frame, or proscenium, served to separate actor from audience for the first time in the history of the theatre. Behind this frame a painted, illusory picture was hidden or revealed by a curtain. The original two-dimensional painted picture eventually grew into the three dimensional stage set with the employment of flat wings (at the sides), borders (hung from above), and drops (for the background), all painted on canvas. Borders and wings were suspended on pipes or beams in the supporting gridiron overhead, and were raised and lowered by a system of ropes.

---

* Marcus Vitruvius Pollio, famous architect and engineer, lived in Rome in the First Century B.C. His ten-volume work, *De architectura*, was printed in Rome at some time between 1453 and 1490. Copies of this early edition are in the Morgan Library and Columbia University Library in New York. The 1495 edition, printed in Venice, is in the Parsons Collection of the New York Public Library.

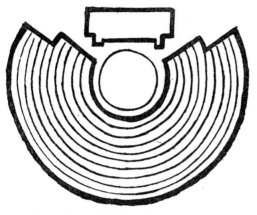

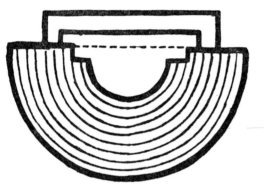

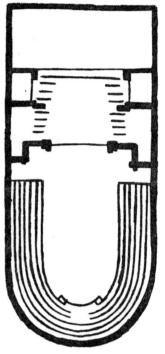

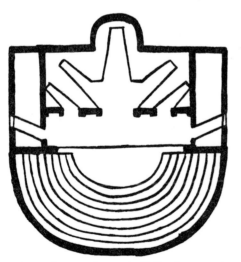

1 Greek theatre (Epidauros)

2 Roman theatre (Aspendos)

3 Renaissance theatre (Palladio theatre, Vicenza)

4 Court theatre (Teatro Farnese, Parma)

5 Italian box opera theatre (Teatro alla Scala, Milano)

The development of the theatre from the Greek amphitheatre to the Italian box opera house.

Gridiron and traps provided machinery for the various miracle effects necessary to the mythological plots; they also proved enormously useful for Grand Opera. The actual stage floor rose slightly from front to back to conform with the perspective design of the scenery. The dim glow provided by candle or oil lamps, mounted as foot, wing or border lights between the flat sections of scenery, helped to blend the various painted areas into one illusory three-dimensional stage picture.

The two concepts of amphitheatre and perspective picture were essentially contradictory. The classical semicircular auditorium had worked best with a shallow stage. Now the spectator wanted to see into the distant depths of the perspective scenery, and a new auditorium design was required to make this possible. The next logical step, therefore, was the reshaping of the semicircular auditorium into a rectangular, elliptical or horseshoe form. We can see this transition by comparing the theatre of Vicenza with the Teatro Farnese at Parma.

The Italian box opera house

When the public was admitted to an opera performance for the first time at the Teatro San Cassiano in Venice, in 1637, the amphitheatrical rows of seats which characterize the private Teatro Farnese had given way to a new arrangement. Tiers of seats were mounted one above another, and the audience was grouped in boxes around the central box of the sovereign, according to social rank. Only from the royal box could the perspective picture be seen without any distortion. The auditorium was luxuriously decorated, in keeping with the splendor of this aristocratic society.

The Teatro San Cassiano established the typical form of the Italian box opera house. We can still see many beautiful examples of this type of theatre, such as San Carlo at Naples (1737), La Fenice in Venice (1755), the opera house of Giuseppe Galli-Bibbiena at Bayreuth (1748), and La Scala at Milan (1779). The older stages utilized the system of wings, borders and drops painted in perspective. To the present day the Paris Opéra preserves the traditional French system of *costières* (small slits in the floor running across the entire stage area), which provides great flexibility in positioning the wings. A particularly interesting example of this type of stage is the Drottningholm Court Theatre (1766) near Stockholm, where the original machinery and scenery are preserved intact and are still used in performance today.

21

The traditional opera theatre thus clearly attests to its original function. It was designed to entertain a courtly aristocratic society with a "show" presented as an illusory picture in a golden picture frame. This theatre is far removed from the democratic community type of Greek musical theatre which the inventors of opera had set out to revive.

Although social premises and production requirements have changed radically, the baroque design has remained dominant until our time. Monarchies have given way to democracies; modern industrialism and technology have changed our ways of living and our concepts of art. But in opera house design the only change, essentially, has been one of lighting. Candle and oil lamps were replaced first by gas lamps and then by electric bulbs. London's Covent Garden and the Paris Opéra, it is true, installed balconies in place of boxes, or made the existence of boxes less apparent. It remained for Richard Wagner's genius, however, to create an opera theatre of a radically new kind.

The Bayreuth Festival House Wagner's Festspielhaus at Bayreuth, which he conceived together with the architect Gottfried Semper and built in 1876, incorporates many essentially new features. The auditorium is simple, without decoration. Amphitheatrical rows of seats without arms mount, bench-like, in steep ascent. From every seat there is a completely unobstructed view of the stage. The orchestra has been lowered out of sight; the curtain, which until that time had descended from above, now parts in the center; the auditorium, which previously was partially illuminated, is kept in complete darkness during the performance. Except for one imitation, the Prinz Regenten Theater in Munich, Wagner's revolutionary opera house did not influence theatre construction for some time.

Reconstruction of European opera houses During World War II many of the European opera houses were destroyed, particularly those in Germany. The traditional recognition of the cultural importance of opera led to their immediate reconstruction. An extensive tour through most of the new European opera houses, and active work by the author as director in some of them, resulted in several significant observations:

First, the *auditorium* of the historic Grand Opera houses, such as La Scala in Milan and the state opera houses in Vienna and East Berlin, was reconstructed according to the *original* form. Modern stages were added, often within the original walls, as in Vienna and Berlin; but no historic opera house in Europe was modified by the addition of a new form of auditorium.

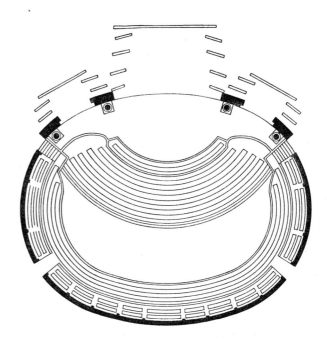

6 A project of the Age of Reason: design for a theatre by Charles Nicole Cochin (1762–65). Inspired by a visit to the Teatro Olimpico, it has a large apron stage and three proscenium openings.

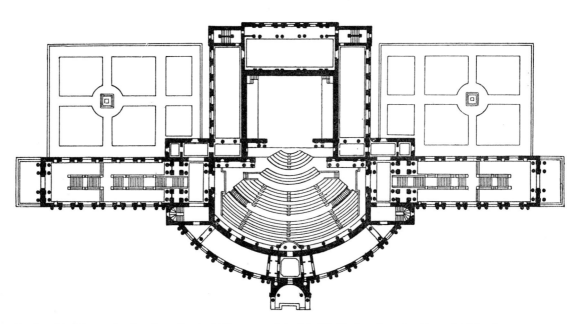

7 Gottfried Semper's plan for a Festival Theatre at Munich (1862), based on the ideas of Richard Wagner.

8　The Festival House at Bayreuth. (From Richard Wagner's "Report on the Laying of the Foundation stone.")

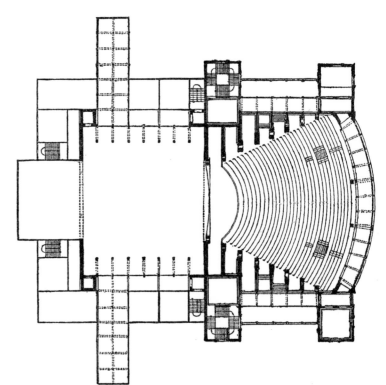

9　Groundplan of the Bayreuth Festspielhaus, built in 1876 by architect O. Brückwald, following Wagner's directions and influenced by Gottfried Semper's plans for Munich.

Municipal opera houses, on the other hand—for example, those in Frankfurt, Hamburg, Cologne and Mannheim—were planned with democratic seating arrangements and improved sightlines. Most of these theatres have only orchestra floor and balconies, as at Bochum and Düsseldorf; while Hamburg (1955) and Cologne (1957) introduced a new type of box. These box designs, probably influenced strongly by the boxes of the Royal Festival Hall in London (1951), are a compromise between the old aristocratic family box, with its real privacy, and the democratic form of balconies. When these boxes are placed at the sides of the auditorium, they provide improved sightlines and therefore make good sense; but when placed in the center of the auditorium, as at Cologne, they satisfy neither functional nor aesthetic requirements. The common observation that they look like sleighs lined up before the start of a race seems quite justified.

In all the new German opera theatres technical facilities are of the first order. But before we discuss this equipment, let us take a parenthetical look at the historic development of operatic stage technique.

Productions in the old baroque opera houses were, as we have seen, based on creating an illusory stage picture which was painted on flat wings, borders and backdrops. The stage area was built twice as high as the proscenium so that scenery could be pulled up out of sight. Often backstage space for entrances from the rear, and some room below stage level for traps, were also incorporated in the design. In the old opera houses the spacial relationship between the "front" of the opera house (the building, including the auditorium, up to the line of the curtain) and the area of the stage was roughly equal, or 1 : 1.

From two to three-dimensional scenery

During the Nineteenth Century a trend towards the use of plastic scenery began. This trend reflected new social and literary ideas, as well as technical innovations in machinery and the invention of electric lights controlled by dimmers. Painted scenery, which had previously been illuminated by candle or oil lamps, appeared shoddy under gas and electric lights, and was slowly replaced by three-dimensional scenery. This new scenery could not be pulled up into the grid, however, and had to be transferred to and from areas situated at the sides, below or back of the main stage.

The three-dimensional scenery was supplemented, quite logically, by a curved cyclorama in place of the old painted sky drop. Such cycloramas were very

From the painted-wing stage to
the built-space stage

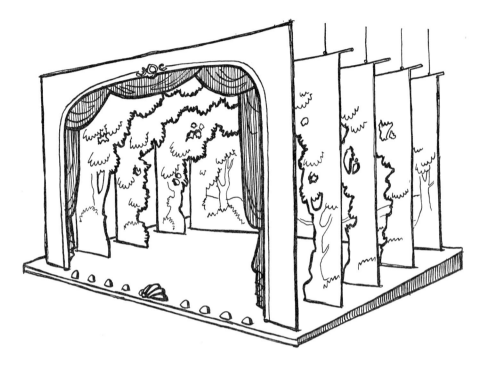

10 Painted-wing stage

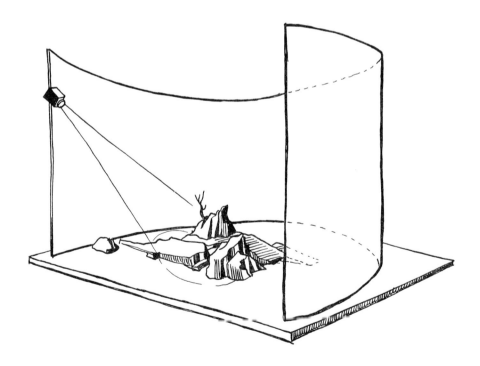

11 Built-space stage (Three-
    dimensional scenery and
    cyclorama)

Technical facilities for
the changing
of three-dimensional scenery

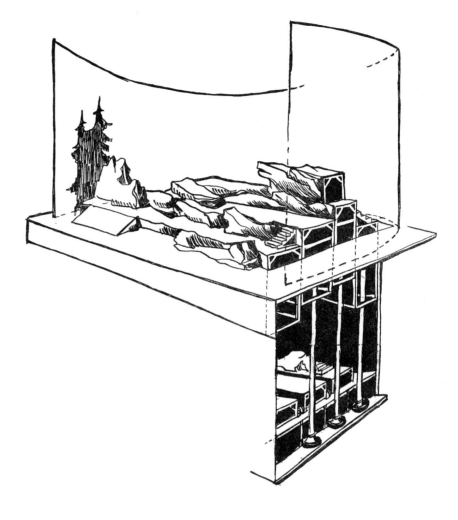

12 Elevator stage

13 Revolving stage

often made of canvas, which could be rolled and unrolled in a vertical semicircle around the back of the stage; or they were constructed of solid material, as at Stuttgart, Venice and the Teatro dell'Opera in Rome. The "panorama" of the Paris Opéra is particularly interesting. Made of asbestos, it is 88 feet high in the center, and can be lifted 56 feet into the grid, completely out of sight.

New stages and machinery The plastic scenery also required new stage machinery. From the time of Wagner we see constant innovations—wagon and elevator stages, double-floor stages and turntables. The need for more space off-stage became imperative. Side stages and big storage areas were added. The average relation between the front of the house and the stage changed from the original 1 : 1 to 1 : 1½ at the beginning of our century. At the present time the ratio is 1 : 3.

The post-war rebuilding of the German theatres provided a field day for German engineers. They responded by contriving the most elaborate stage mechanisms imaginable. Most of the new operatic stages in Europe have (or have provided for) two side stages, a backstage area, elevator-bridges, a turntable, one or more cycloramas (for day and night scenes) and a movable proscenium. The new opera houses in Cologne and West Berlin can be considered models in the application of all these technical facilities. At times, however, there is a tendency to over-mechanization. In Frankfurt, for example, a revolving table thirty-eight meters (123.5 feet) in diameter comprises the entire stage area, leaving no space for the mounting or storing of any scenery but that of the opera actually being performed.

Lighting equipment The development of devices for the convenient handling of scenery was paralleled by the perfection of new lighting equipment. We find highly sophisticated lighting installations in practically all the new theatres. Foot and border lights, designed to light wings and borders, were obviously inadequate. The new treatment of space required carefully controlled illumination of specific areas as well as large sections of the stage. This could be achieved only with an elaborate system of spotlights, floods and projectors, each light responsive to a dimmer at a central board or console. Projection of scenic backgrounds and effects from the front or the rear of the stage onto a straight screen or a curved cyclorama has become a specialized field by itself, the future of which should not be underestimated. Among other artists, Ernest Klausz of the Paris Opéra and Hainer Hill of Berlin have developed particular skills in this technique.

28

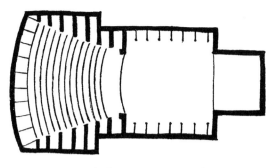

14 Wagner Festival House at Bayreuth

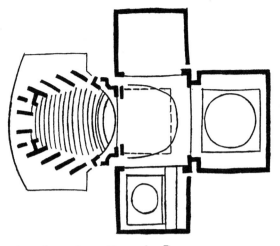

16 Cologne Opera House

The expansion of the stage due to the development of three-dimensional scenery

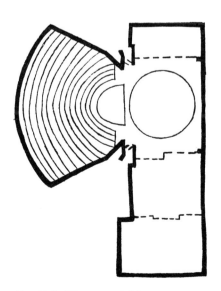

15 Civic Theatre at Malmö

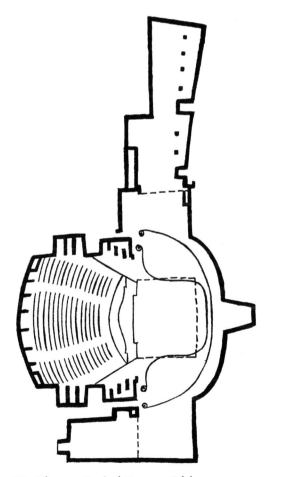

17 The new Festival House at Salzburg

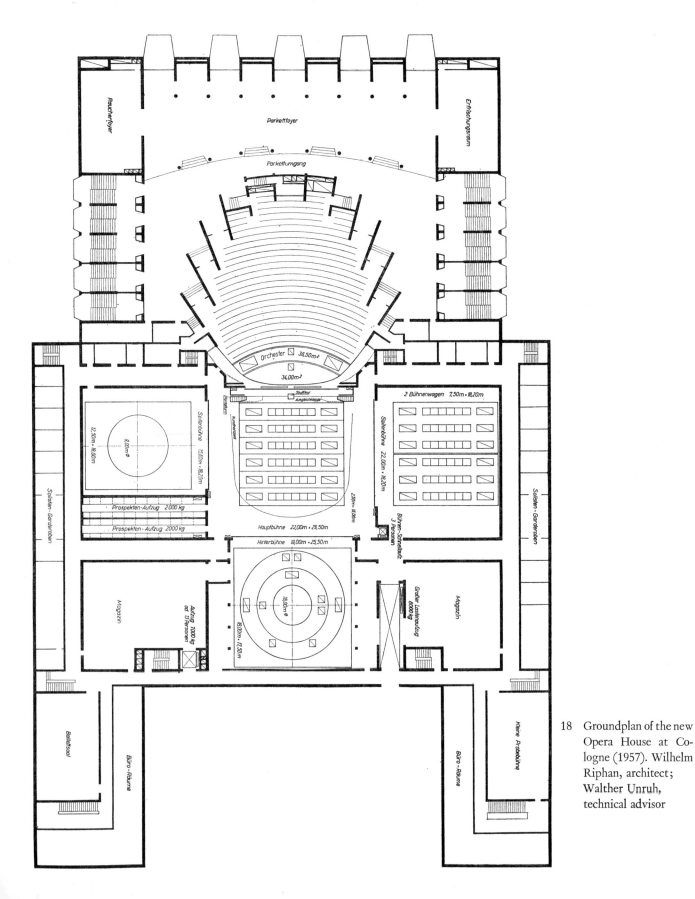

18 Groundplan of the new Opera House at Cologne (1957). Wilhelm Riphan, architect; Walther Unruh, technical advisor

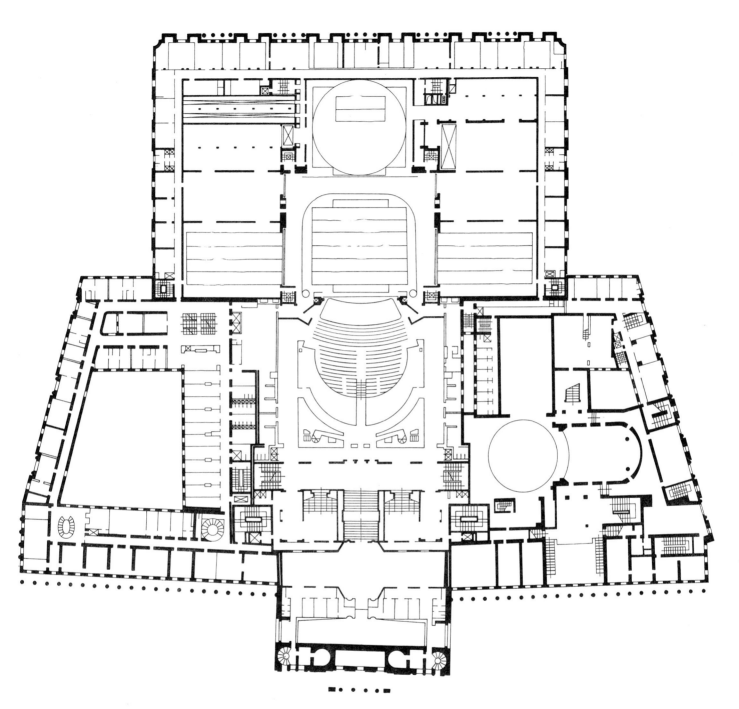

19 Plan for the new Grand Theatre at Warsaw (Teatri Wielki Opery i Baletu), 1957.

German companies, such as Reiche & Vogel, and Hagedorn, both of Berlin, have specialized in various types of light projectors using Xenon lamps. These lamps cover the balanced spectrum of sunlight, leaning slightly to the blue side. They hold the same color temperature under any degree of dimming, thus making it possible to maintain color relationships in scenery and costumes, and in color projections. Siemens & Schuckert have an instructive stage at Erlangen for demonstration of different methods of light control, among them the new low-voltage transistor system which this company recently installed in several of the new opera houses (Düsseldorf, Mannheim).

Many of the new theatres have excellent placement of light-control booths as well as stage direction booths (Hamburg, Münster, Mannheim). These are often located in a main control room at the rear of the auditorium (Münster and Mannheim). In several installations duplicate consoles make it possible to control light from either the auditorium or the stage (Hamburg). Electronic sound equipment is becoming of equal importance (Vienna, Hamburg, Frankfurt), and closed television circuits facilitate communication within the theatre and help coordinate off-stage music with the conductor (Vienna, Munich, Mannheim).

Modern backstage facilities

A great deal of thought has gone into the functional planning of rehearsal halls, workshops and storage areas for scenery, costumes, wigs and props. Every new theatre has its own workshops. As early as 1911 the old theatre of Stuttgart had evolved a very practical layout for the working inter-relationship between the two stages, the scene docks, the workshops and costume storage, and the administration. The new German theatres (Cologne and Mannheim, for example) offer still more instructive examples of efficient methods of operation. In these theatres the same careful study has been carried over into the design of public areas and facilities, such as entrance halls, foyers and wardrobes.

While the physical equipment of the new European opera theatres is for the most part exceptional, much less is evident in the way of new approaches to the basic relationship between audience and stage, particularly in the nerve-center—the proscenium. Reinhardt's Arena Theater in Berlin (1919) advanced in a new direction, but uncompromising new projects have for the most part remained on the drawing boards of modern architects.

Projects for flexible theatres

A Congress and Theatre Exhibition held at Darmstadt in 1955 presented many

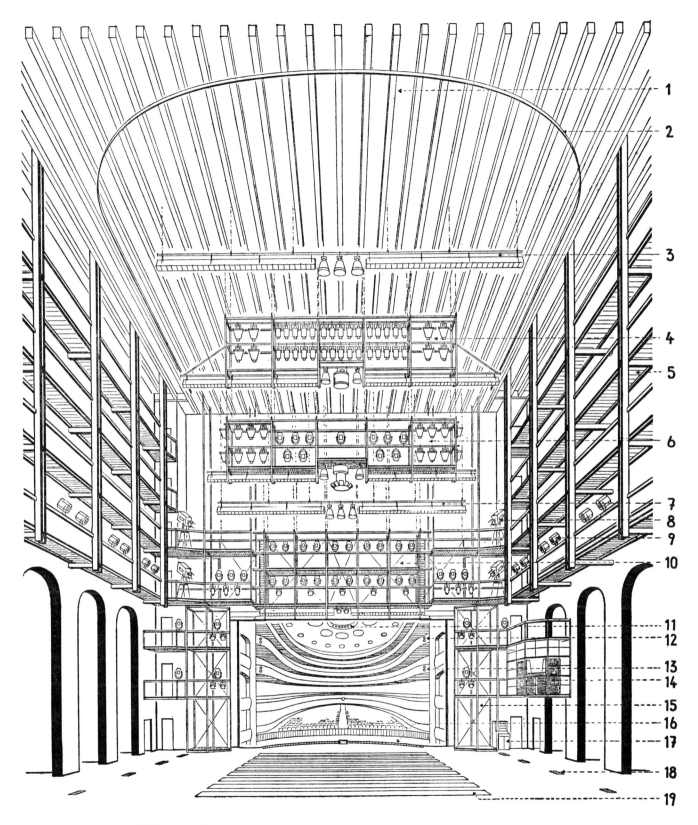

1
2
3
4
5
6
7
8
9
10
11
12
13
14
15
16
17
18
19

20 Arrangement of lighting equipment

promising ideas. Projects ranged from Gropius' famous "Totaltheater" (1927), Ottmar Schuberth's Space Theater (1937) and Gutzeit's "Idealtheater" (1945), to Mies van der Rohe's plan for Mannheim and Scharoun's design for Kassel. The Swiss architect Roman Clemens pioneered ideas for a highly flexible theatre. Erwin Stoecklin, in collaboration with Laban, suggested a "round-theatre" project in which the stage surrounded the entire auditorium. In this plan, the auditorium itself is mounted on a turntable, and during the performance the audience is turned to face successive scenes which are staged on the circular ring. Of particular interest are the designs of the Zurich architects W. Frey and J. Schader, who proposed a convertible theatre project for the Municipal Theater Contest at Basle in 1953. The ideas of the Zurich architect Ernst F. Burckhardt should also not be forgotten in this connection.

These advanced projects go back for their inspiration as far as Cochin (1765) and Morelli (1780), whose reform projects were influenced by the ideas of the "age of reason." All these modern projects envision a theatre without proscenium, or provide a flexible combination of theatre-in-the-round and proscenium stage.

Two exceptions But tradition has proved too strong an obstacle in Europe and not one of these projects has been carried out. Only the little theatre Sant' Erasmo in Milan, built in 1953 as the first permanent European arena theatre by the architects De Carli and Carminati, and the small house in Mannheim, look toward more adventuresome theatrical possibilities. Mannheim's smaller auditorium, by a flexible and simple arrangement, can be changed from a proscenium-type theatre to a kind of two-sided theatre-in-the-round. It also has another interesting feature. The entire ceiling area over the auditorium is equipped with hidden pipes from which scenic elements can be lowered into any part of the house.

But these are exceptions. While we find many interesting architectural experiments, such as Alvar Aalto's asymetric auditorium in his project for Essen, or Alain Bourbonnais' French provincial theatres, European stages in general adhere to the baroque concept, keeping audience and stage apart. There is only a kind of flirtation with the proscenium area to provide some flexibility in the orchestra or forestage zone and in the proscenium itself. Nearly all new theatres, for instance, have the floor of the orchestra pit divided into sections mounted on elevators. The orchestra area can thus be raised in whole or in part to stage

34

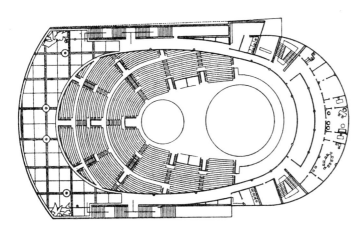

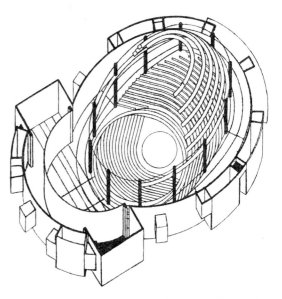

21 Plan for the Meyerhold Theatre at Moscow, 1925; Barchim and Wachtangow, architects. The scenery is changed by a system of turntables in view of the audience.

22 Project for a "Totaltheatre," designed by Walter Gropius for Berlin, 1927. By turning the central part of the auditorium, the theatre can be used as either a proscenium or an arena stage.

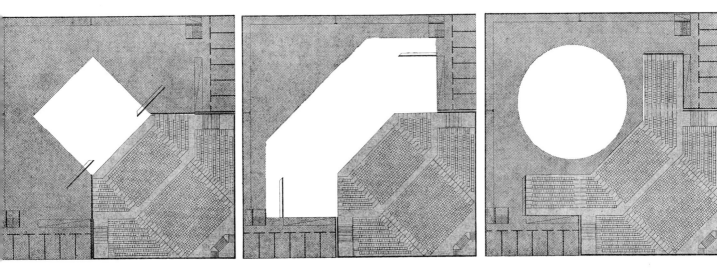

23, 24, 25 The project for the Municipal Theatre at Basle, Switzerland, by the Zurich architects W. Frey and J. Schader (1953). By sliding back the proscenium and side walls, the theatre can be changed from a "peep-hole" to a "space" theatre.

level to provide a forestage. In this respect Bochum has an interesting feature. The iron curtain is placed between audience and orchestra, and shutters in the ceiling of the forestage hide iron pipes. Thus hung scenery can be used in the apron-zone. At Augsburg, also, we find a movable proscenium of considerable technical ingenuity.

Clemens Holzmeister's new Salzburg Festspielhaus has a movable proscenium which allows the width of the stage opening to be altered from about 46 to 100 feet, by means of *Lamellen*, or sliding panels. Some theatres (Malmö, Théâtre Chaillot in Paris) also have provisions to vary the size of the auditorium itself through the use of sliding walls or panels.

In general, however, except for technical devices designed to achieve a minor degree of flexibility, no new concepts have been applied in practice. Nor, does it seem, has much thought been given to problems of television transmission from the opera theatre.

Sizes of European opera theatres Let us note in passing that the progressive solution of the relationship between auditorium and stage should not have been a difficult problem for the new German theatres, considering their modest sizes: Cologne, 1,360; Mannheim, 1,200 for the larger theatre, 600–800 for the small house; Hamburg, 1,650; Vienna Staatsoper, 1,658 seats and 551 standing room. The largest seating capacity is actually no more than 1,800, at the Staatsoper in Berlin.

These figures are interesting in view of architect Werner Kallmorgen's contention* that the following dimensions of a theatre auditorium are to be considered maximum: approximately 85 feet wide and 100 feet deep, with a stage opening 50 feet wide. He believes that "the upper limit of theatrical experience with its personal contact lies, in contrast with film and television, at 1,500 spectators."

In France, England and Italy many opera houses are much larger. The Paris Opéra seats 2,150, and Covent Garden, 2,000. La Scala in Milan seats 2,800; the Teatro dell'Opera in Rome, 2,500; the Teatro San Carlo in Naples, 2,200**;

* *Op. cit.*, p. 6.

** Although the San Carlo Opera House has a larger auditorium than La Scala, it has fewer seats, due to the fact that it has no gallery. There are 180 boxes, and 700 seats in the orchestra.

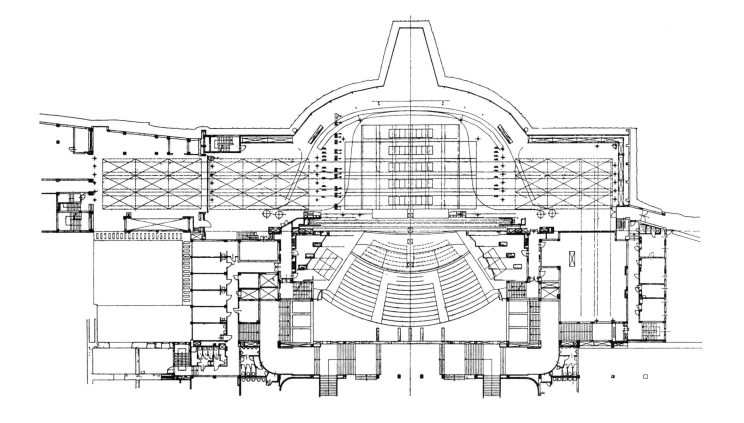

26 Groundplan and section of the new Festival
House at Salzburg (1960)

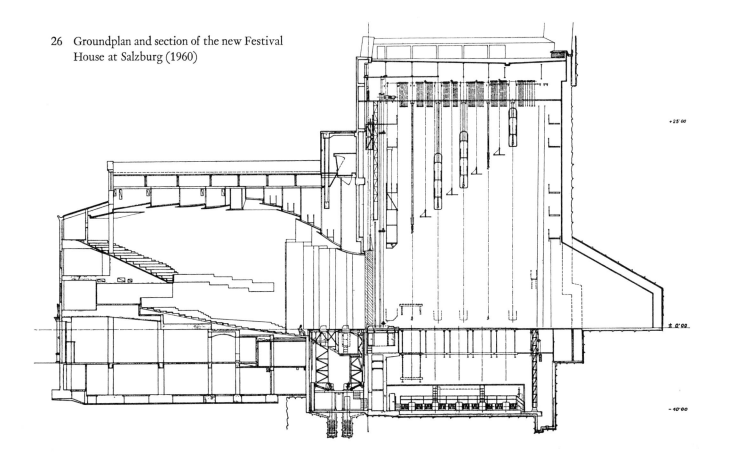

+25'00

± 0'00

- 10'00

and the Teatro La Fenice, in Venice, 1,600; while Florence's modern Politeama or Teatro Comunale, now being rebuilt, originally held 2,500. Italian outdoor theatres range from Verona's Roman Arena, which seats 25,000, to the modern Arena Flegrea in Naples, which seats 10,000. (A remarkable fact is that no amplification is necessary in these enormous outdoor theatres.) The remaining parts of the ancient Teatro Grande in Pompeii seat 3,000; the smaller theatre in Pompeii, 1,200; and the amphitheatre there holds 10,000.

New features in Swedish theatres Considering the great attention given the new German opera houses, it is surprising that the Swedish theatres have not excited more interest. Malmö has a civic theatre, built in 1944, which has many unusual features. By means of plywood walls at the sides and back, the size of the auditorium can be reduced from 1,700 to 1,200 or 800 seats; or even to 500, when the boxes and additional sections of the sides are cut off. In front of the main stage is a large forestage protruding twenty-eight feet into the auditorium. This forestage can be raised or lowered in four parallel sections. The proscenium walls can be adjusted to provide an opening from thirty-nine to sixty-two feet.

In addition to a revolving table sixty-five feet in diameter, the Malmö stage has a system of wagons which run on rails laid in the stage floor, making it possible to roll complete sets directly to the two side stages and the adjoining storehouse. The side stages and the storeroom can be separated from the stage by soundproof iron curtains. With this arrangement, scenery can be built, painted, stored and moved on-stage in one direct communicating system. There is no complicated machinery below stage level; an economical and safe handling of scene shifts is guaranteed. There are excellent provisions for lighting control from the auditorium. The main house can be used for public meetings by opening the rear wall between the orchestra and the foyer, and in another part of the building there is a small "intimate" theatre. Thus, in every important respect the Malmö theatre can be considered a truly fine example of modern community theatre design.

Just as stimulating is a visit to another Swedish city, Göteborg. Here there is an Art Center combining in one building complex an excellent concert hall, a museum and a municipal theatre. The simple beauty of these structures is astonishing. Exquisite marbles and woods are used, and the best Swedish painters and sculptors have done their part. In addition, we find a very interesting technical system which employs revolving, sliding and elevator stages. Wagons run on rails, as at Malmö, but at two levels. This makes it possible to set up and change seven complete scenes, in addition to several smaller ones, simultaneously. The stage has a solid cyclorama.

The most recent Swedish theatre project—and the most forward-looking—is the design by Sven Markelius for Stockholm's new City Theatre, soon to be built.* This, and the small house in Mannheim, are the only theatres in Europe which achieve a flexible relation between auditorium and stage without any compromise.

The basic concept of the opera house has not changed

In summary, we conclude that with few exceptions the traditional concept of the European opera theatre has not changed essentially over the last 350 years. Technical improvements have been made, but the basic character of the baroque opera house has carried over. We still have the passive relationship between audience and operatic performance, and essentially the same methods of production. Opera has remained the illusory picture which, removed from the audience by the separating proscenium, is achieved with a maximum of mechanical devices.

Progressive minds

Forward-looking artists from time to time have recognized the unproductive

* See illustrations 40 and 41.

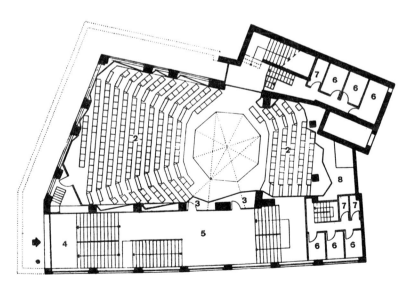

27 The Teatro Sant' Erasmo at Milan (1953); De Carli and Carminati, architects. This is the only permanent arena stage in Europe.

direction of this road, which looks to the past instead of the future. At the beginning of our century, Adolphe Appia was the first to raise his prophetic voice.* Then, in 1906, Georg Fuchs thundered: "Today's extreme development of stage machinery and with it the consequential naturalism have led the peep-show stage *ad absurdum*. We have reached the end of our wisdom. The development of our conventional theater itself has proved to us that the entire peep-show stage with wings and borders, with backdrops and setpieces, with footlights and gridiron, is superfluous; that here we drag along with us an apparatus which excludes any unfolding of true modern art. Therefore, away with the gridiron! Away with the footlights! Away with the setpieces! And away with the backdrops, borders, wings and wadded tights! Away with the peep-show stage! Away with the box theater! This entire make-believe world of pasteboard, wire, sackcloth and tinsel is on the verge of collapse."**

And such an eminent practitioner as Alfred Roller, the stage designer of Gustav Mahler's operatic productions at the Vienna State Opera, a compatriot of Schönberg and the architect Adolf Loos, wrote in 1909:

"Cyclorama, plastic scenery, moving panorama, turntable, moving stage, pneumatic air, electric light and all other so-called 'technological achievements of the modern stage,' which are praised in such superabundance, and have excited press and public, are actually nothing more than disguises of the old wing stage. The evil began with the 'closed set,' and from that point on we had no choice but to drain the cup to the dregs and to exhaust to the end all the possibilities which this stage offers. Therefore, not reform of the stage, but *reform of the theater!* The solution is, in the main, to renounce the silly tricks and bad taste (called 'tradition') to which we have become accustomed, and to acquire again a living theater on the stage of which everything has admittedly only *significance*—not reality or pretension of reality. Theoretical discussions will not bring us nearer this goal, but industrious work and countless serious efforts will."***

* Adolphe Appia, *La mise en scène du drâme Wagnérien* (Paris, 1895). *Idem, Die Musik und die Inszenierung* (Munich: F. Bruckmann, 1899).

** Georg Fuchs, *Die Schaubühne der Zukunft* (Berlin and Leipzig: Schuster & Loeffler, 1906).

*** Alfred Roller, "Bühnenreform?" An article in the magazine *Merker*, December, 1909.

28 The theatre at Epidauros.

29 The Teatro Olimpico by Palladio, at Vicenza (1585).

30 The first opera proscenium, in the Teatro Farnese at Parma, built by Aleotti (1619).

31 The Italian box theatre:
La Scala in Milan.
Built in 1778, it was
reconstructed in 1946
according to the original
design.

32 The Vienna State Opera
as it looked before its
destruction during
World War II.

33 The Civic Theatre at Malmö, Sweden (1944).

34 The Municipal Theatre at Bochum; Gerhard Graubner, architect.

35 The new Civic Theatre at Gelsenkirchen (1959). Werner Ruhnau, Ortwin Rave and Max von Hausen were the architects.

36 The auditorium of the opera house at Cologne (groundplan on page 30), with its characteristic boxes.

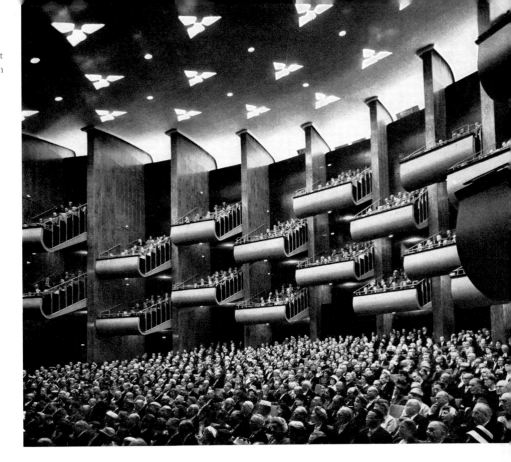

37 The auditorium of the new Festival Theatre at Salzburg (1960); Clemens Holzmeister, architect.
(Groundplan and section on page 37.)

38

39

The project for the new Civic
Theatre for Stockholm,
by Sven Markelius, architect.

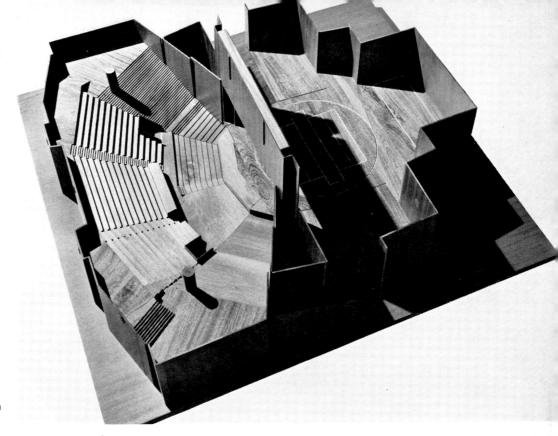

40 Model showing its use as a
    proscenium theatre.

41 Model showing its use as an
    arena theatre.

◄

38 Project for the opera house at
    Essen, by Alvar Aalto. The
    plan shows a new asymmetric
    treatment of the theatre.

39 Theatre project by
    Alain Bourbonnais for Caen,
    conceived as a pattern for a
    French provincial theatre, to
    accommodate the production
    of drama, opera and ballet.

42 The flexible small house of the
National Theatre at Mannheim (1956),
being used here as an arena stage.
Gerhard Weber was the architect.

43 The Realistic Theatre in Moscow
(1933).

Modern technical
equipment.

44 View through the
elevator stage
towards the
auditorium of the
Vienna Burgtheater.

45 The revolving table is
prepared for rehearsal
or performance at the
Vienna State Opera.

46 Opera in the Roman Arena at Verona (*Carmen*, Act I).

48 A production of Verdi's *Otello*, presented in the courtyard of the Ducal Palace in Venice, in the summer of 1960.

▶

(The three productions shown in plates 46, 47 and 48 were staged by Herbert Graf.)

47 *Don Giovanni* at the Felsenreitschule at Salzburg, 1953. Scenery is by Clemens Holzmeister.

49 Adolphe Appia's design for the second act of *Walküre* (1925).

Pioneers of modern opera production.

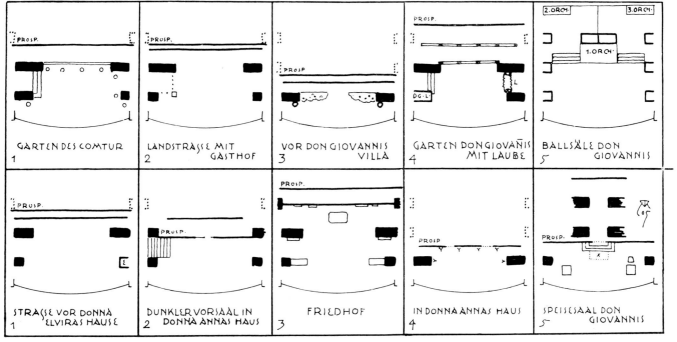

GARTEN DES COMTUR 1	LANDSTRASSE MIT GASTHOF 2	VOR DON GIOVANNIS VILLA 3	GARTEN DON GIOVANNIS MIT LAUBE 4	BALLSÄLE DON GIOVANNIS 5
STRASSE VOR DONNA ELVIRAS HAUSE 1	DUNKLER VORSAAL IN DONNA ANNAS HAUS 2	FRIEDHOF 3	IN DONNA ANNAS HAUS 4	SPEISESAAL DON GIOVANNIS 5

ZWEITER AUFZUG

50 Alfred Roller's layout for *Don Giovanni* (groundplans for the entire production).

51 Act I, Scene 1—Garden of the Commander.

Four scene designs

52 Act I, Scene 3—In front of Don Giovanni's palace.

53 Act II, Scene 3—Cemetery.

54 Act II, Scene 4—In Donna Anna's house.

55
Mario Sironi's
design for Verdi's
Don Carlo,
at the Florence
May Festival,
1950.

56
Gianni Vagnetti's
design for Verdi's
Aroldo, Florence
May Festival 1958.

Oratorios in ▶
staged versions

57
Handel's *Heracles*
at La Scala, 1958.
Scenery by
Piero Zuffi.

58
From the first
scenic presentation
in Europe of Bach's
*Passion according to
St. Matthew*,
Palermo, 1960.
Scenery is by
Veniero Colasanti
and John Moore.
(Both of these
productions were
staged by
Herbert Graf.)

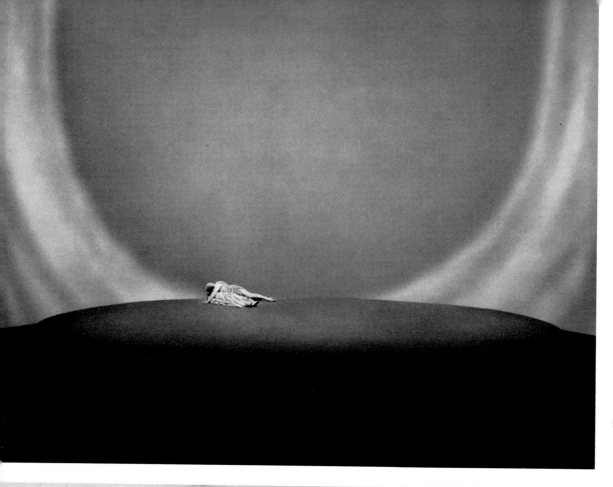

59 Wieland Wagner's production of *Siegfried* at Bayreuth, 1958.

60 Teo Otto's design for Strawinsky's *Renard*; Hamburg State Opera. The production was staged by Guenther Rennert.

3. ARTISTIC POLICY

Stability of the European opera companies

Government sponsorship, and often ownership, of theatres enables the European opera director to operate on a basis of stability. The season in mid-European countries runs usually ten and one-half months. Contracts are written not only for the entire year, but often for several years in advance, and pension funds are established for old age. In Italy, where the main season begins in December and ends in May, the larger theatres have provided year-round employment for orchestra, chorus and stage hands by adding summer activities such as concerts or opera.

With a subsidy taking care of about half of his expenses, the operatic manager is in a position to plan his artistic program with some imagination. He does not have to stick to bread-and-butter operas in order to be certain of a well-filled auditorium. He can vary his familiar fare with a stimulating selection of operas from earlier periods; better still, he can produce modern operas. On one survey trip, I heard, during a period of three weeks, the following works: Alban Berg's *Lulu* (Hamburg); Hindemith's *Mathis der Maler* and Janáček's *Cunning Little Fox* (Wiesbaden); Handel's *Jephta*, in a scenic production, and Orff's *Antigonae* (Stuttgart); Werner Egk's *Revisor* (Schwetzingen); Orff's *Trionfi* (Vienna); and Schönberg's *Moses and Aaron* (Zurich).

Opera in the language of the audience

Except for London's Covent Garden, operas are normally sung in the language of the audience, since understanding by the public generally takes precedence over any aesthetic principle. Only at festivals, such as the June Festival in Vienna or the festivals at Salzburg, Glyndebourne and Amsterdam, did I hear opera sung in the original language when the language was foreign to the audience. More recently, however, the Vienna State Opera, under Herbert von Karajan, has been producing Italian operas in Italian, and the Zurich Stadt-theater, under my direction, now presents operas in the original German, Italian and French, taking advantage of the extraordinary fact that all these languages are spoken and understood in Switzerland; they are, in fact, the principal national tongues of the Swiss Confederation.

Same orchestra for opera and symphony

In most Continental cities the opera orchestra is also the symphony orchestra. In Europe, as opposed to America, opera orchestras developed first. Later these same orchestras began to give concerts. That explains why the two regular weekly concerts (or more accurately, the public dress rehearsal and one concert) of the Vienna Philharmonic Orchestra are given on Saturday and Sunday afternoons—the orchestra is busy at the opera house every evening. In Milan and Naples the symphony season precedes and follows the opera season.

Opera production in Europe is organized on two different bases. There is first the repertory system, under which a large number of operas are staged and repeated throughout one or more seasons. There is also the *stagione* system, under which a work is performed for a relatively short time, after which another work takes its place. In the latter case one opera may alternate with one or two others—but for a limited part of the season.

Repertory system

Obviously the repertory system, which predominates outside Italy, demands a permanent ensemble of singers to insure continued quality of performance. A shortage of first-rate voices is making this increasingly difficult for the leading opera theatres. All of them draw on a relatively few "name" singers who appear practically everywhere. The day when Vienna, Dresden or Frankfurt had permanent ensembles of soloists is over. On a study trip through Germany I heard Leonie Rysanek sing within the space of ten days in Berlin, Cologne, Stuttgart and Vienna, while Maria Callas was upsetting the politics of Milan, Vienna and Rome.

Stagione system

The *stagione* system, traditional in Italy, avoids this ruinous situation. It keeps the original company of soloists intact for the short period during which one opera is being performed. This system is not accepted in the mid-European countries. They follow the repertory system theoretically, but performances suffer from deteriorating standards because in practice the casts are changing constantly and are insufficiently rehearsed.

The same "guest" technique is followed by the leading stage directors. For instance, Günther Rennert was billed as producer of the *Magic Flute* in Hamburg, Berlin, Frankfurt, and Vienna. Conductors and designers move around with equal alacrity. Only small stages with singers not in general demand are free from this artistic calamity. On the other hand, these houses tend to suffer from a general inferiority of vocal quality which, particularly in Germany, is disturbing. Only this situation, however, made it possible for many fine young American singers to find employment on European opera stages—an arrangement that worked out well for all concerned.

58

The repertory system employed by the leading opera houses results in deterioration because of the lack of permanent ensemble. Only festivals, which exhaust the run of their repeat performances within a short period, are able to keep up artistic standards. On the other hand, the festival idea itself has frequently been degraded. The first opera festivals—the Bayreuth Wagner Festival, in existence since 1876, and the Salzburg Festival, centering on its own Mozart since 1922—still have unquestionable individual distinction. So have some relatively new ones, like Glyndebourne. But now festivals are sprouting in such numbers and are exchanging the same leading artists in such a manner that frequently they turn out to be merely high-priced tourist attractions. Only the Italian outdoor summer opera productions (Verona, Rome, Naples and others) are designed to offer opera primarily to the people who by their own tax money made them possible.

Modern standards of production Operatic stage production in Europe has reached high levels, particularly in German-speaking countries. Of course we find distinguished productions in England, Italy, France, Sweden and the Netherlands as well. Perhaps at times German stage directors tend to go to intellectual extremes, working over productions with a sense of *Gründlichkeit* (thoroughness) which can be exhausting to people more direct, but nobody can deny the artistic inventiveness and technical skill many of these productions demonstrate. Of course, plenty of rehearsal time, and the fact that scenery and costumes are for the most part entirely new, provide the necessary premises for such fine work. Felsenstein's operatic productions at the Komische Oper in East Berlin, for example, profit by painstaking preparation throughout several months of rehearsals devoted to a single opera.

The most interesting observation for us, however, lies in the evident contrast between the over-mechanization of the new mid-European opera stages and the production requirements of today's leading stage directors and designers. The reopening of the Vienna State Opera in 1955 provided a curious lesson in this respect. Six stage directors, among them myself, and five designers were invited to prepare seven new productions for the occasion. The new stage offered every mechanical device conceivable, yet not one of us exploited the equipment.

The Wagner brothers Most uncompromising among operatic directors of today is Wieland Wagner. In his productions at Bayreuth, he and his brother Wolfgang have followed the path marked out by the visionary theories and designs of Adolphe Appia, who more than fifty years ago renounced naturalistic stage mechanisms in favor of imaginative use of space and lights. A great part of Appia's work is now in trust at the Museum of Art and History in Geneva, where he lived. For this reason I went there, and found my effort richly rewarded. His grandson, Edmond Appia, who is in charge of the Appia Foundation, let me have copies of several articles which have remained unpublished until the present.

The following quotation from an essay entitled "How to reform our mise-en-scène," written in 1900, appears here in print for the first time: "Stage production, like other processes of art, deals with forms, light and colors. Well now, these three elements are in our power, and consequently we are free to handle them in the theatre, as elsewhere, in an artistic manner. Until now it was commonly believed that the mise-en-scène ought to attain the highest possible degree of illusion, and it is this principle (unaesthetic if there ever was one!) which has condemned us to stagnation."*

Today, fifty years later, this idea has become the creed of modern European opera producers. The German theorist Siegfried Melchinger has defined it as the "concentric theatre" (the theatre which focuses on the essential significance).** Today's directors tend to employ simple scenic constructions with a few plastic pieces set against curtains, gauzes or cycloramas. Light is supreme; it outlines the acting space and follows the movements of the singing actor. The dramatic action, simplified and concentrated, dominates the stage. All this reflects Appia's thesis: "An object is rendered plastic to our eyes only by reason of the light which strikes it, and its plasticity can be given artistic value only through artistic application of the light; this is self-evident."***

A new concept of operatic production has emerged, a concept in striking contrast with the old system employing endless stage mechanisms. This new approach no longer aims at naturalistic imitation, which the movies can accomplish so much better. Rather it strives for imaginative re-creation of the mood of the music through abstract elements—space, light and gesture.

* Translated by the writer from the original French.
** Siegfried Melchinger, *Theater der Gegenwart* (Frankfurt: Fischer Bücherei, 1956).
*** Adolphe Appia, from the same essay cited above.

4. OPERA SCHOOLS

Historic relationship between
opera company and conservatory

A very interesting relationship often existed in times past between the great opera companies and the leading music conservatories, both government-sponsored. Richard Wagner recognized the importance of establishing such a working relationship as essential to his program for the reform of operatic stage production. In 1865, in a lengthy "Report on a German Music School to be established in Munich," he states:

"The art of interpretation, which was exercised and preserved at the conservatories, stemmed originally from the great music institutes in which the most important artists of the nation personally worked and created. The conservatories of Naples, Milan and Paris received and cultivated what the theaters of San Carlo, La Scala and the Académie de Musique before them had developed in collaboration with the taste of the nation, arriving at authentic classic form through actual performances."

The national opera houses originated the style; the conservatories or music schools "conserved" it. Leading composers, conductors, stage directors and singers participated actively in these schools as performers as well as teachers. From my own experience as a student at the State Academy of Music and the Performing Arts in Vienna, I can attest to the value of this kind of relationship. The conductor and stage director of the student performances in which I participated were no less than the leading conductor and stage director of the Vienna State Opera.

Curriculum

Today European conservatories still concern themselves primarily with comprehensive musical study on a purely practical professional level. Academic instruction, per se, is ordinarily provided by music departments of universities. The curriculum for the opera singer at the Paris Conservatoire National de Musique, for instance, distinguishes between "Vocal Training" (five years, including an elementary course in technique and an advanced course in interpretation) and "Lyric Art" (three years of dramatic study for opera or opera comique, which is open to the students of the advanced course in Vocal Training). Students of "Lyric Art" study *solfège*, vocal ensemble, fencing, body training, phonetics, piano, make-up, acting, speech and history of music. This work is climaxed by a course in which entire operatic roles are coached. The final examinations are public. The best students in the Lyric Art course remain for one month under option for engagement at one of the national opera houses.

The historic Music Conservatory of Naples preserves a division between the "School of Singing" (five years) and the course in "Declamation and Scenic Art" (two years). The latter course consists of the following program:

First Year

a) Theoretical knowledge of the essential qualities and requisites of the artist.

b) Exercises in reading and pronunciation.

c) Declamation.

d) Beginning of interpretative study of drama, tragedy and comedy.

e) History of the theatre and costume.

Second Year

a) Study of melologue.

b) Study of parts of tragedies, dramas and comedies of the classic and modern masterworks of both the Italian and foreign theatre.

c) Elementary studies in coordinating singing with action.

d) Studies of parts of operas and their interpretation.

e) Biographical studies of composers whose works the student interprets; historic studies concerning the origin of certain operas and the personalities involved.

f) Various exercises and ensemble scenes.

The training of the opera singer at the State Academy of Music in Vienna requires six years of vocal studies, the last two of which are paralleled by dramatic instruction at the Opera School.

Richard Wagner's proposal for reform of opera schools

While these historic conservatories have maintained to the present day a curriculum aiming at thorough professional instruction, they seem to have lost living contact with the opera houses themselves to a great extent. Richard Wagner, in the report mentioned above, proposed a reform of the traditional conservatories. He planned to establish a new kind of music school, which would revive and modernize the active relationship between the school and the masters of the opera theatre. Referring to the apprentice system in vogue during the classic period of Italian painting, he proposed to his protector, King Ludwig II: "The studio, the workshop of the Master, while he is creating and bringing to light his works, is the true school for the chosen disciple. To give such a workshop also to the musician of our time, be this the beautiful goal of the noble friend of my art."

In his proposed conservatory, Wagner wanted to include a course in singing, with instruction in voice, speech and declamation; a course in drama, with an assistant teacher of declamation and a ballet master; a course in music theory, harmony and analysis of form; a course in piano playing; and an orchestra course emphasizing ensemble playing. The curriculum would be based on performances of classic works and progress gradually to modern works. He even suggests that the school should collaborate with the private teachers of the city for the purpose of individual instruction and common public performances.

Wagner's proposals were never realized. But when he became master of his own theatre, he outlined a plan for a "School for Singers and Conductors" at Bayreuth in connection with the performances of his works. The plan included a training course of nine months each year for two years. The first year was to be devoted to general musical studies, the second to the interpretation of his own works. This training program was to lead to practical participation in the performances of his works during the third year. The Study Seminar which Richard Wagner's grandsons instituted in 1954 and the Master Classes established by Friedelind Wagner in 1959 are still far from achieving Wagner's great original concept.

On the other hand, a program which includes a comprehensive course of training leading up to the performance of opera, with the student working in active contact with a leading operatic organization, has been developed by several European schools.

Opera school in collaboration with the opera house

The Royal Music School at Stockholm has an opera class where I heard some extraordinarily fine voices. This school functions in close collaboration with the opera house. It is administered by a governing board, on which director and staff members of both the opera house and the school work together. The students pay no fee and are given seats to opera performances free of charge. The thorough curriculum consists of scenic dramatic song (study of roles), stage performance, ensemble singing, diction, reciting, piano, harmony, music theory and ear-training, declamation, history and aesthetics of music, history of the theatre, plastic movement and dance, make-up and mask design, Italian (compulsory), French, English and German. Two performances are given each year: one at the Academy, and one, with orchestra, in the opera house.

La Scala in Milan has its own "Scuola di Perfezionamento Artisti Lirici." For admission to the school the student must appear in a final audition before a committee composed of the General Manager and the Artistic Director of La Scala, as well as the Director of the Conservatory of Milan, among others. In course of time, according to his qualifications, he is gradually worked into the regular performances at La Scala.

The most interesting example of a European operatic training center working in collaboration with a professional opera house was the "Centro di Avviamento al Teatro Lirico" (Center for Advancement to the Lyric Theatre), which operated at Florence from 1937 until 1944, when the theatre was destroyed in the war. The director of the Center, Mario Labroca, was also artistic director of the Florence Opera House and the musical director of the school, Mario Rossi, was the chief conductor of the Opera House and the Symphony Orchestra. The staff of teachers included a maestro for voice, a maestro for the study of roles, an assistant conductor, a stage director and a teacher of speech (recitation). For the men there was an instructor in fencing; for the women, an instructor in dance.

Operatic productions were given, both preceding and following the regular opera season, using the orchestra and chorus of the Florence Opera House. One group of productions was presented during October and November, and the other during April and May. Five operas were performed during each period, and each opera was presented three or four times. Great artists like Stabile (Falstaff) and Pertile (Otello) sang leading roles; all the other parts were taken by students from the Center. The best students were also used in minor roles at the May Festival and as understudies for every part. All students were allowed to attend rehearsals of the regular opera company.

The directors of the Italian opera houses were invited to attend the fall productions of the second-year students. If they found a particular student promising, he was no longer obliged to take part in the tasks prescribed by the general curriculum during the second year, but instead was coached and prepared in those parts which his future director requested.

The idea of the Florentine operatic training center was, in some respects, revived by the present Teatro Lirico Sperimentale (Experimental Lyric Theatre) of Spoleto. Since 1947, the Teatro dell'Opera of Rome has presented four or five operas during the month of September in the lovely Teatro Nuovo of Spoleto, primarily to train young opera singers. The organization is under the supervision of the artistic director of the Rome Opera House, which also makes available its orchestra, chorus, ballet and stage technicians. The students are prepared in Rome during the regular opera season under the guidance of conductors from the Opera House and a prominent stage director.

This experimental opera season was founded "with the approval of the Presidency of the Council of Ministers as an institution for professional advancement in the lyric theatre for young Italian singers, who, having completed their vocal studies, have not yet made a stage debut." *

The Experimental Theatre of Spoleto has collaborated successfully with the American Commission for Cultural Exchange with Italy. A great number of Fulbright singers have regularly taken part in preparing and performing Italian operas there. The leading roles of the last opera presented during each Spoleto Experimental Theatre season are usually entrusted to young American singers, and I had an opportunity during my visit to convince myself of the excellent account they give of their work. The singer I heard in the part of Butterfly was later engaged as a leading soprano at the Hamburg State Opera. Will the others find similar opportunities?

Except for these notable efforts, there is little active contact today between opera house and school. But this is not a serious problem in Europe, since there are so many small opera companies. They offer the promising young professional training through actual performance—and without too great damage to either his fledgling reputation or the sensitivities of his audience.

* From the official program of the Teatro Sperimentale at Spoleto.

5. OPERA IN TELEVISION

Our picture of European opera would not be complete without a general review of the role played by the government-supported European television networks. According to Kenneth A. Wright, who until 1956 was Head of Music of the British BBC Television Service, this company has presented since 1946 "sixty-five operas and operatic programs ranging from ballad opera to Chisholm's twelve-note, grisly one-acter, *Dark Sonnet;* from Offenbach to Menotti, Donizetti to Richard Strauss. During that time the number of adult viewers in Great Britain has grown from fifty thousand to over eighteen millions, one-quarter or one-third of whom normally tune into a televised opera. Presentations have ranged from programs of excerpts to full-length productions; interestingly enough, the latter consistently the more popular." *

In the Milan studios of the Italian television network, full-length operas are produced, frequently with prominent Italian conductors and singers. France presents televised opera occasionally, while in Germany television opera is advancing at a quick pace. More recently Austria joined the European television family and has presented notable productions, while the Schweizer Fernsehen in Switzerland is just beginning to include opera in its programming.

European production methods differ

It is interesting to note that European methods of operatic television production on the whole differ very much from those employed in the United States. Only in England are operas always staged in studios, expressly for telecasts, with live sound. The young singers there sing in English. In London I saw kinescopes of two opera telecasts—Menotti's *Saint of Bleecker Street* and Strauss' *Salome.* These were both excellent productions by Rudolf Cartier.

Italy

The Italian television works in a different manner, as I know from my own experience, having staged studio telecasts of *Falstaff* and *The Marriage of Figaro* in Milan. The Italians use the "playback" method, in which a master tape recording of voices and orchestra is made first (this tape is later used for radio broadcasting). During the telecast the original artists act and sing the roles while listening to a playback of their own voices; the sound actually going over the air comes from the pre-recorded tape.

* Kenneth A. Wright, "Television and Opera," *Tempo,* autumn issue, 1957 (London: Boosey and Hawkes Ltd.).

The German television studio at Munich carries the playback system a radical step farther. As in Italy, the sound is recorded in advance by regular opera singers. In the actual telecast, however, well-known stage and film actors act the roles, "mouthing" the words as the pre-recorded sound is broadcast. I saw a full-length kinescope of *The Marriage of Figaro* in Munich, and I have to admit that while I do not agree with this procedure for artistic reasons, the producer, Kurt Wilhelm, achieved a feat of quite unbelievable technical skill.

Television transmission of operas directly from the stages of European opera houses is handicapped by poor technical conditions: unfavorable location of cameras, insufficient lighting and general lack of preparation for this purpose. *Cavalleria Rusticana*, as transmitted from La Scala, and my own productions of *Aida* and *Carmen*, telecast from the Arena in Verona, were unsatisfactory as television productions because of these technical shortcomings.

Equally unsuccessful was the telecast of the opening performance at the reconstructed Vienna State Opera in 1955. On this occasion the opera was *Fidelio*. During the first two scenes (the yard and cell of the prison), the television screen was wrapped in Stygian darkness. The other extreme was reached at the opening of the 1957 San Carlo Opera season in Naples, when I staged Boito's *Nerone*. The second act requires the mystery of a dark stage, with spotlights creating all kinds of magical effects. This act was ruined for the audience in the theatre by the glaring television lights, which washed out the original stage lighting completely. A more successful transmission was a performance of Werner Egk's *Revisor*, staged by Rennert and presented by the South German Television from the charming theatre at Schwetzingen.

The BBC Television Service was the first organization willing to undertake the expense and make the effort required to achieve a satisfactory solution of the difficult problem of theatre telecast. For its annual transmission of an actual performance from Glyndebourne, the BBC invites a special audience. This audience understands the problem, and the television director can thus make changes in the camera positioning and the lighting, as well as carry out the other adjustments necessary for a technically satisfactory telecast. The result delights the television viewer at home, while not annoying a paying audience in the theatre.

The generous attitude of the Teatro Massimo in Palermo and of the Italian

Television Network made possible a successful transmission of the first European scenic presentation of Bach's *Saint Matthew Passion*, which I staged at Easter, 1960, with Dr. Hermann Scherchen as conductor. The television technicians were present during the last rehearsals of the production. Then two days were put at their disposal, during which they could suggest the necessary technical adjustments, in consultation with the television director and myself.

At an International Conference on "Opera in Radio, Television and Film," which was held during the Salzburg Festival of 1956 under the auspices of the Austrian Radio and the International Music Council of UNESCO, a world-wide group of television experts presented a comprehensive picture of the status of opera in television and film. This successful conference was followed by another on "Opera and Ballet in TV and Film" in 1959. At this conference the different production methods used in Europe and America were demonstrated.

Limitations

It was clear that the new medium of television, at least in its present stage of development, transmits realistic action and intimate scenes very successfully. Opera as an absolute art form, however, and particularly opera on a large scale, appears to much less advantage. A great part of the operatic literature, including Wagner, does not seem suited to this medium as it now exists.

The successful examples of opera telecasts from the studio were taken for the most part from intimate, realistic operas, comic operas, or modern musical theatre. The Munich TV productions of *Die Kluge* and the *Comoedia de Cristi Resurrectione*, by Orff, seem to be exceptions in this field, because they have as their aim the visual translation of emotional values. Apparently the co-operation of a composer with an outstanding director, G. R. Sellner, brought about the miracle in this case.

Operatic films

Operatic films shown at the 1956 conference revealed the same tendency to restrict productions to realistic works. Among them were Menotti's *The Medium*, a Japanese production of *Madame Butterfly*, and the Russian *Boris Godunoff*. Felsenstein's film of *Fidelio*, however, proved that applying a realistic technique to opera that was not conceived in this style can have unhappy results.

A beginning in opera documentaries was made by Paul Czinner's film of my *Don Giovanni* production at the Salzburg Festival of 1954, with Wilhelm Furtwängler conducting. The film was a serious attempt to "catch and preserve the palpitating and sustaining magic of a great live performance, in spite of the

68

unyielding conditions of a stage production." And it was to prove that "a genuine film of high technical quality can be achieved within the confines of the theatre."* Czinner and his sponsor, I. R. Maxwell, applied the same approach to a documentary of the Bolshoi Ballet filmed at the Covent Garden Opera House. The 1960 Salzburg Festival production of *Der Rosenkavalier* is the third of these films.

Technical problems European television has not yet solved many of the technical problems peculiar to operatic telecasts, such as the handling of color values and the placement of the orchestra in live performances. Studio performances usually must be mounted in limited space, but there is frequently ample rehearsal time available. The Italian TV, for instance, allots to each opera about one full week of studio rehearsals with cameras. This is a very generous amount of time, since the playback method frees the producer from consideration of acoustical problems, and permits the singers to concentrate entirely on acting.

Government sponsorship It might be well to note here that the European television companies are not only government-sponsored, but work without any other competing networks, with the exception of the British commercial television network and a second network expected in Germany. Transmission is on a nationwide basis, and, in general, the opera production is the only program on the air at that time.

There exists a European Broadcasting Union, which, through an international exchange center for television programs called "Eurovision," occasionally makes programs produced in one country available for transmission in other countries. Union difficulties often hamstring such exchanges, however. At the present time union restrictions bar the use of pre-recordings in England and limit the transmission of Italian kinescope films of operas.

The new television quarters in Berlin and the new studios of the BBC in London have several interesting features. In Berlin wagons carry scenery from the storerooms on a moving belt running before the cameras. At the London studios the orchestra is mounted on elevator platforms. The director can thus bring the orchestra into camera range at will. But only at Hamburg are plans being made for the production of "live" television opera in the presence of an audience.

I have seen many excellent television productions of opera in London, Munich

* Paul Czinner, "The Idea behind the Film," from the printed presentation and program of the film *Don Giovanni*.

and Milan, but I have not seen any really new solutions to the production problems of opera on television. A specialized television theatre for music-dramatic presentations, with a proper relation of orchestra and audience, has not yet been created; nor has transmission of opera from actual performance in the opera house been solved. Furthermore, no constructive collaboration between opera companies and television has been established, although this should not be too difficult in Europe, considering the fact that both organizations are sponsored by the government. Here, unfortunately, we enter the field of human frailties and personal jealousies, a time-honored tradition as well as a peppery stimulant at many European institutions. Finally, no operatic and educational films made especially for television seem to be in prospect at this time.

Conclusion

In summary, these are the major factors which characterize opera in Europe:
1. Opera in Europe is solidly entrenched in historic tradition. It is recognized and subsidized by governments as a cultural obligation to the citizenry, and it therefore has a secure existence and organization.
2. This official support has made possible imaginative and artistic programming. It has also helped develop methods of production which have reached a high degree of technical perfection.
3. At the same time, European operatic production has remained bound by old traditions, built up over 350 years. European opera is fundamentally tied to the concept of the baroque Court Opera. It has not developed the new approach necessary to meet the changes in modern society and technology.
4. For these reasons, European opera must be evaluated in its own historical setting. We will do well to study carefully the highly accomplished European achievements, but we should not assume that the European way is the only way to organize and produce opera. We cannot expect to uproot European opera and transplant it bodily to the United States, because the conditions which lie behind opera production in Europe are entirely different from the conditions in America.

Let us now take a close look at opera in America.

Part II. Opera production in the United States

1. SPONSORSHIP

After finishing my European study, I returned to the United States in June of 1957. Immediately I had occasion to notice how different conditions are on the American side of the water. I was about to realize an old dream of mine—to stage a production of Wagner's *Walküre* in the magnificent Red Rocks Theatre on the slopes of the Colorado Rockies.

Some American approaches to opera production

On the way to Denver for rehearsals, I stopped first at Cleveland to visit the Musicarnival tent theatre. This proved to be a remarkable experience. An audience of nearly 2,000 had gathered under the canvas top to see a performance of a musical comedy in theatre-in-the-round style. These shows were being put on every night during a three-month summer season, at moderate prices. Due to the form of the theatre, no one in the audience was more than fourteen rows from the stage, with the last row only forty-four feet back. In addition to popular Broadway musicals, this theatre had produced *Carmen* and *Tosca*, in a modernized version by John Gutman. The operas were received with such enthusiasm that the producer, John L. Price, has since presented other operas. From Cleveland I crossed Lake Erie into neighboring Canada to attend the Shakespeare Festival at Stratford, Ontario. Here, on the site of the former tent theatre, a permanent building of unique design had just been completed. This building continues the tradition of the old English theatre, carrying the action into the auditorium without a proscenium. An audience of 2,176 filled the house to capacity; most of them had made the trip by car from considerable distances. The theatre had cost roughly $1,500,000, half of which had already been sub-scribed by individuals and corporations all over Canada, with the inhabitants of Stratford contributing a good part of it themselves. The program of the Festival included concerts and opera as well as legitimate theatre.

From Stratford I went to Salt Lake City, Utah, since I had heard from my friend, Maurice Abravanel, Musical Director of the Utah Symphony, that he was conducting three performances of *Salome* for the annual Summer Festival. I was impressed not only by the performance, but by the attendance as well. Each night some 5,000 residents of the Mormon city filled the Stadium bowl for this unorthodox opera and were so stunned by the shocking ending that no one dared to applaud for some time after the end of the opera. Collaboration between the University, the Symphony and various local artists, who filled all the roles except the three leading parts, proved eminently successful. The University of Utah has sponsored this Festival every year since 1948, presenting one opera and one musical each summer.

I saw another aspect of the American operatic scene at Santa Fé, New Mexico, where the personal initiative of a young conductor, John Crosby, has resulted in a new opera season of sophisticated distinction in a new theatre built especially for the purpose. The Santa Fé repertory included not only standard works like *Madame Butterfly* and *The Barber of Seville*, but operas like Strauss' *Ariadne auf Naxos*, Strawinsky's *Rake's Progress* (the composer himself was present for the preparation of this), and a modern American opera, *The Tower*, by Marvin David Levy. What an unusual experience to hear also *Così fan tutte* in this charming open-air theatre, seating 500, on the San Juan Ranch outside Santa Fé, with the lights of the atom city Los Alamos shining in the distance!

And so I went on to Denver and the nearby Red Rocks Theatre, where the Denver Symphony, under its musical director Saul Caston, presented Wagner's *Walküre*. The all-American cast included both leading Metropolitan Opera stars and local artists, who sang the Walkyries. In addition, there were girls riding horseback, and other girls stationed on top of the gigantic rocks that rim the natural amphitheatre. At the end of the opera the United States Army provided a "magic fire" that would have delighted Richard Wagner. And he would have liked not only the fine voices and youthful enthusiasm of his Colorado Walkyries, but also the happy response of the audience of 7,000 who attended each of the two performances despite obstinately truculent weather.

Opera in commercial summer tent theatres-in-the-round, opera resulting from teamwork between university and local symphony, opera sponsored by private donors, opera presented by the local symphony for local audiences—these are all new approaches to the presentation of opera, unknown to European tradition. They point to the existence of new, vital possibilities for operatic production in the United States. Let us take stock of them.

The first impression we receive when we survey the total American operatic scene is one of wide-spread growth and activity. Every conceivable type of organization is now putting on opera. These groups range from established opera companies to music clubs, from professional to educational and amateur groups, and they produce everything from Grand Opera to the simplest of children's operas. The annual surveys carried out by *Opera News** demonstrate the rapidity of this growth. During the twelve months ending October 15, 1953, there were 386 groups producing opera. In 1956, there were 600, and in 1959, there were 727. During the same seven-year period the total number of opera performances in America rose from 2,704 in 1953 to 3,953 in 1959.

It is true that most American operatic groups give only a few performances, utilize very simple production techniques, and have very modest private financial support. But the rapidly-increasing interest in opera as expressed by the figures is sufficient proof of dynamic growth in this field. Why is it, then, that opera in the United States is not supported financially as in Europe, and has not reached the standards of production which it enjoys there? A rapid review of operatic history in the United States will help us answer this question.

Grand Opera

At the time when baroque opera (from which stem the European traditions of sponsorship and production) was flourishing in Europe at the sophisticated courts of absolute monarchs, the settlers on the North American continent were battling for existence in their struggle to establish a new life. Their political concepts were based not on monarchies, but on democratic self-government. Their music was not Grand Opera, but simple Puritan hymns, folk songs and ballad operas.

During the Nineteenth Century the age of modern industrialism began, and in America a certain standard of living was established. The families who

---

* *Opera News*, published by the Metropolitan Opera Guild, New York. No. 2 (1953); no. 3 (1954, 1955, 1956, 1957, 1958, 1959).

became wealthy through the rapid industrial growth of the country after the Civil War took over the role of the European emperors to some extent, and sponsored the importation of European Grand Opera.

The Metropolitan Opera was founded in New York in 1883. Originally the opera house was owned by the occupants of the boxes of the "Diamond Horseshoe." During this historic chapter, Italian opera was imported from Milan, German opera from Vienna and Berlin, and French opera from Paris. Performances were given in the original languages, with the original casts, costumes, sets and staging. In this manner Grand Opera was established not only in New York, but also in Chicago, Boston, San Francisco and other major cities. This procedure of importing opera from Europe under private sponsorship continued with minor variations for many years.

Following the depression of 1929, however, and the decline of private fortunes, the Metropolitan began a process of democratization under Edward Johnson. The first radio broadcast, which took place in 1931, brought opera to millions of listeners across the country who had never heard anything like it before. The Opera Guild, which enlisted public support, was founded by Mrs. August Belmont in 1935, and the opera house was purchased by public contributions in 1940. Many American singers were successfully added to the roster, and some operas were performed in English. This modernization has continued, particularly in the field of production, under Rudolf Bing. Despite these changes, however, the basic policy of the Metropolitan Opera remains the same: It is today, as in the past, the foremost American stronghold of European Grand Opera produced in the original styles.

The San Francisco Opera Association has maintained a similar tradition on the West Coast, although the strictly European concepts followed by its founder, Gaetano Merola, have been modernized by Kurt Herbert Adler. In Chicago's Lyric Opera as well, the original intention of producing European Grand Opera has prevailed.

The Metropolitan Opera

The crux of the matter is this, however: There exists no system of American sponsorship corresponding to the European government subsidy. Even the Metropolitan, which has always enjoyed a certain unique position, is by no means free from economic headaches even though it was granted a tax exemption by Congress in October, 1951. This amounted to a yearly bonus of approximately

$550,000, the amount of tax paid during the last season the government required it. The Metropolitan is also greatly assisted by increasing contributions from the Opera Guild as well as from individual sponsors. The total amount of private subsidy, including revenues from fund-raising campaigns during the seven seasons from 1950 to 1957, has averaged about $500,000 per season.

But even the operating losses of $553,383, $610,025 and $711,419, which were incurred during the three seasons between 1955 and 1958, are not nearly as large as the subsidies granted by many European governments to their leading opera houses. These operating losses cover a season of some twenty-four weeks in New York, with the house filled to within 93 to 97 per cent of seating capacity. This amounts to an over-all loss of about $3,500 per performance, during the Company's New York season and seven-and-one-half-week tour. Without the tour, which is profitable, the deficit would be larger. Obviously the annual loss would be much greater if the season were to be extended to a year-round operation, in the manner of the major Central European opera houses.

Nevertheless, compared with other American opera companies, the Metropolitan is in an enviable position. It has nationwide prestige, contributions from frequent public campaigns, support from the Opera Guild and the National Council, and an annual income of about $500,000 accruing from radio, television and recording operations, building rentals and such. During the 1958–59 season the operating deficit of $528,873 was, for the first time since the 1946–47 season, exceeded by annual contributions, and the year ended with a surplus of $3,150. This season also saw the establishment of a Metropolitan Endowment Trust.

Far less endowed both in operation and financial support are the other opera companies in the country. The Metropolitan Opera in 1959–60 gave a total of 236 performances of twenty-four operas during a total season of thirty-two weeks, twenty-five of these weeks in New York. The San Francisco Opera during its 1959 season put on sixty-five performances of fourteen operas within ten weeks, of which only six were spent in San Francisco. Howard K. Skinner, Manager of the San Francisco Opera and Symphony Association, informs us that the City and County of San Francisco contribute $15,000 to the Opera Association and $10,000 to the Symphony annually. In addition there is a guarantor system which Mr. Skinner explains as follows:

"Persons occupying seats in the Boxes, Orchestra and Grand Tier sections of

The San Francisco Opera Company

the house on the Regular Series must sign a guarantee under which they can be assessed up to a given amount toward any deficit at the end of the season. A guarantee is not required for the upper portions of the house, nor does it apply to any seats for repeat performances of the operas. Both the Symphony and Opera Associations conduct annual fund drives, during which time contributions are accepted from corporations and smaller businesses, as well as from private individuals." *

Chicago's Lyric Opera

Chicago's Lyric Opera, which reinstated Grand Opera at Chicago in 1954 after an absence of many years, began with a still shorter season. The number of performances has grown from eighteen during the 1954 season to twenty-seven in 1959, when a seven-week season was given.

Like the Metropolitan, the Chicago Opera depends on private sponsorship of its new productions. The *Report of the Lyric Opera of Chicago, 1958*, states that "gifts of entire productions by both individuals and foundations have made possible major new productions of two of America's leading opera companies. Lyric Opera must receive comparable consideration if it is to continue its record of splendid accomplishment." Carol Fox, Lyric's general manager, has termed "a significant new Production Fund and the establishment of a permanent Endowment as the most vital needs for Chicago's growing resident opera company." The *Report* continues, "Operating an organization such as Lyric Opera successfully without capital funds presents almost unsurmountable difficulties; furthermore, no long-range artistic plans can be made. Chicago is justifiably proud of its great Symphony Orchestra and its Arts Institute, and has endowed them richly. Our resident Opera, with its brilliant record, must be permanent in the same way."

In 1957, the Chicago company was able to cover its operating loss of approximately $250,000 through private contributions. But the future of the Company obviously depends on continuing efforts to obtain private financial support, and success in building up its newly established Endowment Fund.

In its 1959 season the Lyric Opera established a new precedent by renting

---

* From a letter by Howard A. Skinner. The San Francisco Opera and Symphony Associations are separate organizations. The Opera, however, utilizes Symphony personnel in the Opera Orchestra.

scenery and costumes, for six of the ten operas performed, from Rome, San Francisco and London. From Covent Garden in London they also borrowed the stage director for Janáček's *Jenufa*. The cost of $4,000 for the rental and shipment of the sets and costumes was certainly economical, in view of the expense a new production would have entailed.

Other Grand Opera companies

In addition to the three leading Grand Opera companies, which base their operations principally on foreign "name" artists, there are a dozen other well-established groups throughout the country. These include Cincinnati's famous "Zoo Opera," Philadelphia's Lyric and Grand Opera Companies, the Connecticut Opera Association, the Opera Guild of Greater Miami, the Grand Opera Association of Detroit and others. All of these continue the tradition of European Grand Opera. Grand Opera in America, however, has not received governmental sponsorship in the European manner.

Grand Opera not increasing

There has been an enormous growth of interest in music, and particularly in opera, during the past thirty years. This development began during the Depression and simultaneously with the growth of broadcasting and recording. Yet the number of Grand Opera companies which have continued the production of opera in the traditional manner, and the extent of their activities, has *not* increased up to the present. Grand Opera in Chicago was actually suspended for several years. Boston lost not only its traditional season of Grand Opera, but its opera house as well. The truth is that at the present time, when the existence of literally hundreds of small opera groups gives vivid testimony to the lively interest in opera, there is, outside the Metropolitan, no other major company in continuous extended operation; nor are any of them performing on a basis of financial sponsorship secure enough to guarantee its artistic future and the livelihood of its employees.

Community Opera

A new development

During the Second World War, European artists were unable to come to America. Thus the people of the United States were forced into an awareness of their own resources in the operatic field. Young American singers, conductors and composers were given an opportunity to show their worth.

At the same time, civic opera companies were founded. This new type of organization was formed to produce opera professionally on a financially solvent basis; and this meant using local soloists, choristers and instrumentalists in co-operation with other existing local organizations. These companies frequently import one or more "name" singers for box-office appeal, but the basic policy is to keep the production a community activity employing local personnel. Operas are frequently done in English. Box office receipts and other practicalities are decisive, and these considerations limit the possibility of enriching the repertory with modern and, possibly, American works.

Community opera groups in the United States range from well-established companies like the New York City Opera, which gives a fall and spring season of about five to six weeks each, to companies which perform only one opera per season; from companies which operate on a purely professional level, to Opera Guild companies which are sponsored by music schools trying to reach audiences outside the confines of the educational community. There are also touring companies prepared to bring opera to communities or schools which otherwise would not experience a live performance. All of these organizations are trying to find an organic role for opera within the pattern of American community life.

The New York City Opera

As mentioned above, the most notable of these groups, though not the first, historically speaking, is the New York City Opera Company sponsored by the New York City Center of Music and Drama, Inc. This corporation also sponsors the City Center Drama Company, the New York City Ballet, the Light Opera Company and the Art Gallery. The City Center, as it is popularly called, is supported by the City of New York within present political limitations. This means that the City supplies the 3,000-seat house at the nominal rent of $1.00 per year. The deficits of the opera and ballet companies are balanced by profits from the other companies, rentals of the theatre and private contributions.

In addition to private donations, grants have been made to the Center by various foundations. The Rockefeller Foundation, for example, gave $200,000 between 1953 and 1955 for the commissioning of new works in the fields of ballet and opera; and the Ford Foundation contributed $105,000 towards a unique season of ten contemporary American operas during the spring of 1958. This season of American works was scheduled originally for a five-and-one-half-week period, but public interest was so great that the season was extended for an additional week. A further grant of $310,000 was made available for the

78

1959 and 1960 seasons. During these three spring seasons the City Center Opera produced twenty American works, and during the spring of 1960, performed four of them on a five-week tour.

Since its founding, the City Center Opera has given more than 1,000 performances of sixty-four different operas. There were ten American premières of works by living composers. The maximum price level has been held to $3.95. Many young singers have made their professional debut here, and more than thirty singers and conductors have gone on from the City Center to the Metropolitan Opera.

While neither the policy nor the financing of this young company is solidly established—Grand Operas like *Turandot* and *Macbeth*, done in Italian, are presented side-by-side with works of the *opéra comique* type in English, as well as modern works—the City Center Opera Company, presently under the guidance of Julius Rudel, has an indispensable part to play in New York musical life. It also serves as a worthy incentive to other cities thinking of organizing an opera company.

Well-established community opera companies now exist in various parts of the country. We can list here as examples, according to their age, those at Pittsburgh, New Orleans, Boston, Fort Worth and Seattle. These were preceded by organizations such as the Civic Opera Association in St. Paul, which, like the company in New Orleans, was even subsidized in a modest way by its city.

New Orleans and Pittsburgh   The companies at New Orleans and Pittsburgh normally perform six operas during the season, each opera being given twice. "Name" singers are imported for leading roles; the rest of the cast is made up of local singers. The opera orchestra is formed from local symphony personnel. With the exception of the New York City Opera, these groups have more extended operations than any other community operas. A more ambitious production schedule is apparently not possible at the moment; there are problems enough with this program. Pittsburgh confesses its most pressing concern is "finding a theatre and money."

Fort Worth   A similar community group, the Fort Worth Opera Association, performs three operas during the season. Each opera is given twice. Like New Orleans, it enjoys the help of a very active Opera Guild. During the 1956–57 season, 58 per cent of its income was derived from donations, the rest from ticket sales. The

Association considers its major problem to be the establishment of a reasonably dependable method of raising the annual budget. It proposed "licking this problem by undertaking a summer musical series in-the-round, profits from which shall be dedicated to the various cultural outlets in Ft. Worth".

Opera in Houston Since 1956, the lively Texas scene has been enriched as well by the activities of the Houston Grand Opera Association under its general director Walter Herbert. Every season this company presents three operas, giving two or three performances of each. The 1958 season started out impressively with a successful, if radical, production of *Salome* by Rexford Harrower in an English translation. The program was balanced by popular operas sung in the original languages, using casts which included both "name" artists and capable local singers. During the summer of 1957 a free workshop for qualified regional singers was begun. Two free public performances are given each summer in Houston's open-air theatre in Hermann Park. Six of the fourteen operas produced up to the spring of 1960 were sung in English. New scenery was designed especially for several of these productions, employing designers from the Houston area whenever feasible.

In 1956, the Association put on two productions with a budget of $40,000; in 1957, a budget of $80,000 was available for three operas; in 1958, expenses rose to approximately $90,000 for seven performances of three operas, with about $60,000 covered by box office receipts and $30,000 by contributions. In the 1959–60 season, for the three operas produced the budget was raised to about $107,000. One-third of this was covered by ticket sales, two-thirds by contributions.* Serious financial problems, which faced this efficient group at the close of its 1959–60 season, were happily resolved when a total of $75,500 was raised by foundations and individuals for the 1960–61 season.

The New England Opera Theater In Boston, the New England Opera Theater under Boris Goldovsky, founder and artistic director, today provides practically the only means for musical Boston to enjoy opera, aside from the one week of Metropolitan performances and Sarah Caldwell's Opera Group. On a budget raised 60 per cent by private contributions and 40 per cent by ticket sales, this company during the 1956–57

* These figures were supplied by Carl A. Fasshauer, Jr., Business Manager of the Houston Grand Opera Association during those years.

season gave only one opera, *The Secret Marriage*, by Cimarosa. It was sung in English, as is the company's general policy. There were twenty-five performances. In 1960 this organization was in its fourteenth year. The Boston seasons have had from four to twelve performances yearly. "We have no guarantors," writes Goldovsky, "but from the Board of Directors and the sponsors we receive annual gifts of about $25,000. The Leadership Training Program, which permits me to train conductors and stage directors, and also to develop new methods, scenic materials and such, is underwritten by a separate fund.

"Artistically and financially speaking, I have found that touring is the most satisfactory activity. It practically pays for itself and gives the singers a chance to develop the details of their roles in a manner not possible during the few performances of the Boston season. I have come to the conclusion that a combination of a short run in the home town and an extended tour is the most efficient solution, at the present stage of our operatic life."

Similar companies are attempting to establish community opera all across the nation.

Washington, D.C. Opera Society   In Washington, D.C. an Opera Society was founded in 1956. During the short time since, it has had a highly successful career. It undertook a distinguished program of operas, such as *Ariadne*, *The Rake's Progress*, *Falstaff*, *Pelleas and Melisande* and others, despite the fact that lack of an adequate opera house permits recovery of only half the expenses, even when every seat is sold. Collaborating with the National Symphony Orchestra as well as the Washington Ballet, and relying on young professional singers and directors, the Opera Society hopes not only to become established as Washington's official opera company, but also to develop "a National Opera League which would enable the Society to co-operate with other opera companies in the use of sets and artists, and thereby make possible an interchange of performances during a season and increase the range of repertoire throughout the country." Perhaps one day this company will be performing in the National Cultural Center, currently in the planning stage.

Many of the civic opera companies are working along the lines of what we consider the traditional "Grand Opera" concept; in other words, they follow more or less the production styles in which the various operas were first presented. Other companies are trying to develop new production techniques,

81

necessitated frequently by budget limitations. Clear boundaries rarely exist between the two concepts.

The Dallas Civic Opera

As an example of the first approach, the new Dallas Civic Opera tried to orient its first production in 1957 on a strict Milan-Dallas axis. An operatic concert by Maria Callas was given, at $10.00 per seat. Two performances of Rossini's *Italiana in Algeri* were presented. Not only the stars, but also the scenic designs of the original Piccola Scala production were imported for the occasion. A budget of approximately $68,000 was set up to cover expenses, with a deficit of $25,000 anticipated. This deficit, covered by private contributors, was exceeded. No one seems to have been frightened by this initial experience, however, and a more ambitious schedule, with Callas' star shining brightly in the operatic heavens, was set up for the second season.

The young Dallas Civic Company in 1958 produced five performances of three operas during a period of two weeks. By 1960 the program had grown to nine performances of four productions within three weeks. To increase support for the company, Lawrence V. Kelly, the general manager, organized the Civic Opera Guild in 1951. Three years later it had 1,500 members. Financing of the company is accomplished through membership contributions. Members pay $25, guarantors, $1,000.

In the spring of 1960, an exchange agreement with Covent Garden Opera House in London was effected. Dallas sent its 1958 *Medea*, with Callas, to London, together with the Dallas musical director, the major part of the cast, the stage director and the scenic and lighting designers. In return London sent its 1959 *Lucia* to Dallas.

Mr. Kelly explains further: "The cost of this total effort is based on the total cost involved in both transportations, divided evenly in half. May I add that it represented a very substantial saving to both our houses, for these two editions are both more elaborate than average. We hope to continue this exchange with other major European theatres, as it represented an absolute first in the artistic world and proved not only satisfactory and educational, but most enjoyable to the respective audiences.

"Our future plans involve a continued expansion, building a rotating permanent repertoire of approximately fifteen productions, which will be added to at the rate of three each year, and as new techniques and wear and tear appear, replacements will be in order. It is highly possible, given a slow, carefully worked-out plan, that this community can support a major opera season of six or seven weeks, once the hurdles of new production costs are over."

Other community opera companies

Many civic groups recognize the glory of imported names, possibly from the "Met," but their more modest means curtail their desires and ambitions. Still other groups are genuinely concentrating on the problem of young American singers, and use as many of them as possible, at least in minor roles. In addition to organizations already mentioned, Rosa Ponselle with her Civic Opera Company in Baltimore thinks first of her young students, who dream of one day achieving her fame. In Florida, the Opera Guild of Greater Miami, under Arturo Di Filippi, produces opera in the original, and collaborates with the University of Miami. Typical opera groups based on American talent are the Sun State Opera Federation at Tampa, Florida; the opera guilds of Mobile, Alabama and Jackson, Mississippi; and the Civic Opera Company of Shreveport, Louisiana. This last group relies on an income derived 35 per cent from donations, 15 per cent from program advertising, and 50 per cent from ticket sales. The group plans "to use more and more talent from the local area in roles of more importance, to increase the number of productions each season, and to increase the size of our audiences to the point where the company will rely less on gifts from patrons and more on box-office income." They also plan to inaugurate a season subscription plan.

Similar opera groups are springing up throughout the land in every state—in Birmingham, Alabama, for instance; in Chattanooga, Tennessee, where Mr. and Mrs. Werner Wolff have been building up an opera company since 1943; and in Memphis, Tennessee, where opera on a small scale started more recently.

Tulsa, Oklahoma

Tulsa, Oklahoma offers a typical example of how an American community can create opera for itself. The Tulsa Opera Company, organized shortly after World War II, now puts on two performances of two operas each season. It has the full support of the entire community, and covers the annual deficit of about $35,000 with contributions from Supporting, Patron, Sponsor, Contributor and Donor Members, as well as a Woman's Opera Guild. It employs members of the Tulsa Philharmonic Orchestra.

Manager Jeannette Turner writes: "We import the conductor, stage director and artists for the principal roles. Our chorus and all backstage committees (make-up, costumes, props, etc.) are volunteers. We have stressed our educational and scholarship projects because we believe that—particularly here in the Middle West—these are the strong foundations which assure future growth and interest."

These are the things that put the Tulsa Opera among the constructive rather then the simply impresario-type opera groups: educational programs for the singing chorus and ballet, scholarships for instruction in voice and dance, an opera workshop for local talent, and a unique system of two *free* matinee performances for students of junior high school age from Tulsa and the surrounding area. These programs meet with great enthusiasm. The company receives letters like the following, written by a fourteen-year-old student: "As a rule, I do not really enjoy operas. I do not understand them . . . As a result of this performance, I am going to try to change my attitude toward operas."

Opera at Karamu A particularly fine opera project exists in Karamu's musical wing at Cleveland, Ohio, directed by a practical dreamer, Benno D. Frank. Since he joined the Karamu staff in 1948, Frank has staged about seventy operas and musicals. Among these were many American premières, including Bloch's *Macbeth* and Janáček's *Katja Kabanova*. The operas are presented either in a proscenium theatre seating 240 or an arena theatre holding 120. Due to the limited space they are performed with one or two pianos, yet they set a precedent in the sense that even operas rarely heard are presented here a minimum of forty times. Everything is sung in English. Since operas or musicals are presented for ten months a year, every night except Monday, this theatre offers the singers a unique opportunity for frequent repeat performances. I can attest to the fact that productions of Menotti's *Medium* and *Consul* in the arena theatre of Karamu were for me actually more exciting than the excellent original Broadway productions of either opera. Like the other people in the audience, I wanted to jump up from my seat to take the side of Magda Sorel against the secretary of the Consul who was denying her a visa.

At Karamu all racial barriers have been successfully surmounted. Three-quarters of the performers are Negroes, only one-quarter are white. Since Karamu is in many respects a unique institution and has new buildings with facilities for complete operatic training, one hopes that it may obtain the scholarships it seriously needs for further development.

In Detroit, Michigan, there is an active Civic Opera in addition to the old Civic Opera at Flint. This latter group has produced one opera in English every year since 1932. In Chicago the Lyric Opera has an unorthodox counterpart in the "All Children's Grand Opera," which, with children ranging in age from six to sixteen, has performed such ambitious works as *Aida* and *Don Carlo*. (Since this is Grand Opera, it is of course presented in Italian.) We are assured by the enthusiastic founder-director, Zerline Muhlman Metzger, "The performances are serious, more or less artistic presentations *in toto*, with scenery, costumes, unaltered scores, unchanged keys, etc., but not with orchestra."

The Kentucky Opera Association of Louisville produced five modern operas commissioned by the Louisville Orchestra under a Rockefeller Foundation grant. Two operas premièred at Louisville—Liebermann's *School for Wives* and Nabokov's *The Holy Devil*—later met with great success in Europe. Moritz Bomhard, the director of the Opera Association, informs us: "We generally have four new productions each season, which we perform with local singers. On the rare occasions when we imported singers from New York, we found that the advantage of bigger and sometimes better voices does not necessarily make up for the disadvantage of a less integrated performance."

In 1958 Kansas City's Lyric Theater made a successful start. But even important centers like St. Louis, Missouri, or Denver, Colorado, have not solved the problems of supporting a civic opera. Opera at St. Louis has been supplied in the past by the Washington University Opera, which presented some fine performances under Dorothy Ziegler's direction, with support from the St. Louis Grand Opera Guild. Now a reorganization seems to be expected to give civic opera its deserved place in St. Louis. At Denver, a Lyric Theatre under John Newfield's direction is laying the foundation for opera in Colorado's capital.

The operatic horizon brightens as we come to Salt Lake City, Utah. Here the good spirit of Salt Lake, and that of Maurice Abravanel, have joined forces for the benefit of both. Abravanel made his debut as a conductor at the Metropolitan in 1936, with the same production of *Samson and Delilah* in which I made mine as stage director. We shared an equal lack of success on that occasion. Many a night we walked home together discussing opera. Later on, he renounced a successful and lucrative career on Broadway to settle down in Salt Lake City. While his main concern in Salt Lake was the Utah Symphony, of which he is the conductor, he also became Artistic Director of the University of Utah Summer Festival and of the Spring Opera, both of which work in co-operation with the Utah Symphony. In addition he has been responsible for the University's Opera Workshop. With the coordination of these musical institutions guaranteed, he developed the city's operatic activity in a manner which exemplifies how university, symphony and ballet can collaborate for the good of all. At the Summer Festival Abravanel regularly presents opera together with operetta or musical comedy. The combination looks a bit strange at first sight: *Great Waltz* and *Carmen*, *Song of Norway* and *Salome*, *Carousel* and *Rosenkavalier*. But Abravanel explains: "By having a combination ticket at a reduced price for both opera and operetta we have, I believe, brought thousands of people to opera who would not have attended otherwise." The greater total attendance helps to pay the production costs for the opera and also the larger orchestral budget.

In the spring Abravanel produces one opera, using local artists and a smaller orchestra: *Figaro* in 1956, for example, and *Falstaff* in 1960. "All the operas," writes Abravanel, "are sponsored jointly by the University of Utah and the Utah Symphony. We use about fifty-five members of the Utah Symphony . . . The University fully guarantees the Utah Symphony the entire orchestral payroll. In addition, we sponsor, jointly, nine Christmas-week performances of the *Nutcracker Ballet* with the entire Utah Symphony (eighty-one musicians). Since these performances take place during the Symphony season, the Symphony management receives a fixed amount from the University, which makes a handsome profit. All were sold out for the fifth time. In general, the University breaks about even on its ventures with the Symphony. If there is a deficit, the University pays it out of its general budget. For two years out of twelve there was a profit which, of course, the University put into its general fund."

Opera in southern California   Going on to California, we find the Los Angeles Grand Opera Company presenting three or four operas during the spring months. Conductor, stage director and singers are local. There is also the Los Angeles Opera Guild, which not only sponsors the annual visit of the San Francisco Opera Company to Los Angeles, but also produces an opera every spring for the school children of southern California. Performances are presented in collaboration with the Los Angeles Board of Education under a grant of $25,000 from Los Angeles County.

These productions were originally under the artistic direction of Carl Ebert, whose renown is international.

Southern California is bustling with civic opera enterprises from San Diego to Santa Barbara. Most of these activities are struggling and short-lived. There are civic opera groups like those of Santa Monica, Burbank, Riverside and Santa Barbara; there are also reading clubs, like the Hollywood Opera Reading Club and the long-established Euterpe Membership Group. Summer opera is presented from time to time at the Hollywood Bowl, the Greek Theater in Los Angeles and the Redlands Bowl.

To the north
To the north, in Oregon, the Portland Theater Arts Association presents operas; in Seattle, Washington, a Civic Opera Association as well as the Seattle Opera Company are both active.

Across the border:
The Vancouver Festival
Directors of American opera groups, struggling for the most part against financial odds, look jealously across the border into British Columbia. There Vancouver opened its first International Festival in the summer of 1958, with a concert under Bruno Walter's baton. This Festival includes opera. In 1959 a modern theatre was opened with a presentation of Gluck's *Orpheus*. Under the artistic direction of Nicholas Goldschmidt, the Vancouver Festival Society collaborates with the University of British Columbia's Summer School of Arts. The Festival is financed by private subscription, as well as by grants from the Canada Council ($50,000), the City of Vancouver ($25,000), and the Province of British Columbia ($25,000).

Opera at American summer
festivals: Chautauqua, N.Y.
There are, of course, similar festival activities in the United States. Opera was established many years ago at the Summer Festival of Chautauqua, New York, where the Opera Association was considered an essential part of the summer musical season. In 1958 Chautauqua presented its thirtieth season of opera, presenting six different works in English with two performances of each opera weekly during a period of six weeks.

Central City, Colorado
The other old-timer among American operatic festivals is Central City, Colorado. Here, in the lovely, historic opera house of the old mining town, two operas are presented each summer for a period of four weeks. They are new productions employing the best available young singers. All operas are done in English. Among the original aims and objectives of this Opera Association, as stated in 1940 by Miss Anne Evans, its idealistic co-founder, was the plan "to work harmoniously—but in entire mutual independence—with other organizations

which are forwarding music and drama or are trying to gather the early historic data of Colorado; as, for example, the special departments of schools and colleges, symphony and choral societies, schools, libraries, musicians, the managements of town reserves and mountain parks."

At the Red Rocks Theatre

In the magnificent Red Rocks Theatre nearby, the Denver Symphony under Saul Caston's direction presented its first operatic production in 1957—Richard Wagner's *Walküre*. This was followed in 1958 by the first scenic performance of Haydn's *Creation*, staged according to my concepts by Hans Busch and Carolyn Lockwood. The work was repeated in 1959 in Richard Rychtarik's settings and staged by me with the assistance of my son, Werner Graf. We also presented Puccini's *Girl of the Golden West* there, celebrating the centennial of Colorado's Gold Rush.

Within reach of both Central City and Red Rocks are musical institutions located at Aspen and Colorado Springs. These are devoted to higher musical education and appreciation, chamber music and dance. The universities at Denver and Boulder have music departments and opera workshops. Denver, the major city of the area, is growing rapidly, the nearby summer resorts offer unique attractions for tourists, and the entire region seems to have enormous cultural potential. If the noble concepts of Anne Evans can be fulfilled, and a collaboration between the various organizations can be achieved, Colorado will be able to develop the greatest music festival in the nation.

Santa Fé, New Mexico

In 1957 John Crosby established an attractive Summer Opera Festival at Santa Fé, New Mexico. He was not content to restrict the repertory of his new theatre to bread-and-butter operas. With Igor Strawinsky as composer-in-residence, he commissioned and presented new American works in addition to performing established European and American operas. In 1960 he added a training program with Hans Busch as director. Crosby has overcome financial hurdles with taste and patience, and his imaginative policy has brought good returns in prestige as well as attendance.

Opera in the Musicarnival Tent at Cleveland

We find lively operatic activity in many other theatres and festivals all over America. Organizations range from summer theatres sponsored by music schools to music theatre tents, like the Musicarnival tent at Cleveland. *Tosca* was given at Musicarnival in 1957, using an English adaptation by John Gutman. This places the action in "A capital in Eastern Europe behind the Iron Curtain."

88

It remains a matter of speculation whether the new edition was responsible for the success, or Puccini's music, or both; but after a full week of production there was a profit of more than $1,600. This opera was followed in 1958 by a week of *Bohème* performances.

The Empire State Festival   Frank Forest, founder and manager of the Empire State Festival, opened his first season in 1955 at Ellenville, New York. The record proves that he has not compromised on the original idea of the Festival: "It should give works not practical in the commercial theater, it being the duty of the Festival to bring out the best of the new works." He has presented, among other works, Strawinsky's *Canticum Sacrum* and Orff's *Carmina Burana* under Stokowski; and *Elektra* and the American première of Pizzeti's *Murder in the Cathedral* under Laszlo Halasz.

A thunderstorm in the summer of 1958 put an end not only to what was to have been the opening performance, but also to the tent itself. Performances were moved to Carnegie Hall. The following year a new site for the Festival was inaugurated in the Bear Mountain-Harriman State Park, New York, and far-reaching plans were made for modern physical facilities as well as a program for a Music and Art Center. During the summer of 1960 a thunderstorm struck again, damaging the new theatre seriously but failing to daunt the enterprising spirit of the Directors.

Operas are also performed in summer theatres sponsored by music schools or the music departments of colleges. In 1957, for instance, Antioch College, located at Yellow Springs, Ohio, presented Britten's *Rape of Lucretia*, Bernstein's *Trouble in Tahiti* and Strawinsky's *Histoire du Soldat*.

"Opera under the Stars"   At Rochester, New York, "Opera under the Stars," directed by Leonard *at Rochester, N.Y.*   Treash of the Eastman School of Music, has become a regular summer event. This festival had its beginning in the summer of 1953 when local businesses, the Rochester Musicians Union, the Eastman School of Music and the City of Rochester pooled their efforts and produced two performances each of *La Bohème* and *La Traviata* in Highland Park Bowl, free of charge. The casts were made up of young singers from Rochester who were ready for a professional opera debut. Most of them were graduates of the Opera Workshop of the Eastman School of Music. The chorus was composed of singers prominent in local choral groups, who welcomed the opportunity to sing and act in opera.

89

Some 12,000 people filled the Bowl each night during this first season and clamored for more opera the following summer. The City of Rochester appropriated the money. There are normally three weeks or more of stage rehearsal for each opera, after the roles have been coached musically. There are two acting rehearsals with orchestra. Each singer is paid, receiving $150 or less for his role, depending upon its importance; but he receives many times his fee in coaching and practical training in opera dramatics.

California's Redlands Bowl

A similar spirit prevails in California's Redlands Community Music Association's annual music programs presented in the Redlands Bowl, where the public is admitted free of charge. The budget runs to more than $30,000, raised through membership contributions, voluntary offerings at each Redlands Bowl event and income from endowments. For more than twenty years this community project has included opera in its programs.

"Our audiences are largest," comments the founder-president of this organization, Mrs. George E. Mullen, "on the nights we present opera. Whole families come. The 4,500 seats are filled, and the grass is covered with probably an extra 1,500 people. It is thrilling to see parents coming with a troupe of children. They spread blankets on the grass and all settle down to hear the *Marriage of Figaro*, *Così fan tutte*, *Martha*, *Il Trovatore*, or a Gilbert and Sullivan light opera. If the opera is not done in English we have a narrator give a brief synopsis of the story in English."

Lotte Lehmann staged a *Fledermaus* production in the Redlands Bowl in 1957, using singers trained at her Music Academy of the West at Santa Barbara. The following year she presented *Rosenkavalier* with Maurice Abravanel as conductor —an appropriate way to celebrate the seventieth birthday of the world's most famous "Marschallin."

Other summer opera groups

There are, of course, many other summer opera groups. To mention only two more, the Turnau Opera Players have established themselves for the summer at Woodstock, New York; and high up in Maine at Kennebunkport we find the Arundel Opera Theater and Academy of Performing and Related Arts. The Arundel group has been developing an operatic summer theatre and training curriculum since 1948. It now has its own theatre, built with money raised on a bond issue of $35,000 in the surrounding communities. This will be paid off over a ten-year period.

Our picture of community opera would not be complete without a glance at the various operatic touring companies. Touring groups range from the mammoth Metropolitan Opera, which on its annual Spring Tour presents about sixty performances of Grand Opera in various American cities, to the National Grass Roots Opera Company, which was founded in 1948 by A. J. Fletcher at Raleigh, North Carolina, under the patronage of the North Carolina and National Federation of Music Clubs. "In North Carolina," Mr. Fletcher writes, "emphasis continues to be placed on 'Opera in the Schools.' To date more than 376,000 school children have attended Grass Roots performances. All performances are in English, of course."

For some years past opera has been brought to American cities by the NBC Opera Company, which had become well known through its nationwide television performances. Unfortunately, touring did not prove feasible for this group. On the other hand, the Wagner Opera Company tours with familiar works. Another touring company, the New York "After Dinner Opera Company," specializes in operas written on a rather intimate scale; for example, certain Offenbach works. Richard Flusser, who heads up this group, describes himself as "artistic director, general manager, stage director, librarian, press agent, public relations representative, typist, truck driver and general factotum."

It is not my purpose here to give a complete picture of the enormously varied and complex field of American community opera.* In New York City alone, for example, there are a dozen or more semi-professional or training groups. These include not only the well-established Amato Opera Theatre and La Puma's Opera Workshop, but also many new enterprises such as the Community Opera, Actor's Opera, Opera '58 and others. The smaller groups frequently experiment with original approaches to staging. Similar organizations are the

---

* The author asks many friends and colleagues, known and unknown, to forgive him for not mentioning their activities. It is obvious that it would be impossible in this space to discuss all the groups working to promote opera and to provide an outlet for young operatic talent. Complete surveys of companies producing opera in the United States will be found in the lists published by the Central Opera Service (Metropolitan Opera House, New York City). These lists are assembled largely from the files of the Metropolitan Opera Guild's magazine *Opera News*, which publishes each fall an annual survey of American opera. The survey was initiated by the founder-editor of *Opera News*, Mrs. John DeWitt Peltz, and is being continued under her successor, Frank Merkling.

Ansonia Opera Circle in New York and the Opera Ring Association in San Francisco, which present operas in the arena manner.

Many of these smaller operatic groups are essentially experimental in nature. Instead of simply copying European Grand Opera in the original production styles, they want to develop a lyric theatre springing from native American roots, answering local needs and stimulating local talent and sponsorship. None of these groups will assert that they have as yet been able to attain this goal. None will say that they have sufficient financial means to produce opera often enough and well enough. Few have at their disposal a theatre fully adequate for their purposes. Few maintain that they can achieve the production standards they would like. But all insist that the goal towards which they are moving is clear. They want to create an opera organization functioning as an organic part of their cultural community, like their symphony orchestra and music school.

Symphony and Opera

Precedents

I came to the United States for the first time in 1934 at the invitation of Fritz Reiner and Arthur Judson, who at that time was manager of the Philadelphia Orchestra Association. They had asked me to stage a season of ten operas, which were to be presented by the Philadelphia Orchestra as part of the regular subscription series. Every third week the regular concert and its two repeat performances were replaced by opera productions. Two weeks of piano stage rehearsals and one week of rehearsals with the orchestra were available.

This was indeed a memorable season, conducted by Fritz Reiner and Alexander Smallens. Those who heard *Tristan and Isolde* (uncut), *Rosenkavalier* or Strawinsky's *Mavra* played by this famous orchestra, with excellent singing actors and scenery by outstanding designers, or such operas as *Falstaff* and *The Marriage of Figaro* performed in English at the Academy of Music, will not easily have forgotten the experience. There were never enough seats; but, unhappily, managerial problems, such as the availability of the house, the scheduling of chorus rehearsals, mandatory thirty-week contracts for stage hands, the purchase of permanent scenic equipment for amortization in one season, etc., resulted in frayed nerves and a frightening deficit. This noble operatic experiment was thereupon abandoned after only one season, 1934–35.

At the same time the Cleveland Orchestra, under the direction of Arthur Rodzinski, began three symphony seasons which included opera. The permanent stage director, William Wymetal, recalls that during this period the Cleveland Orchestra "presented twelve full productions of opera (four pairs of performances each season) as a part of its regular orchestra series at Severance Hall. A permanent staff, including stage director, chorus director and designer (Richard Rychtarik), was retained under seasonal contracts, and the principal roles were sung by leading Metropolitan artists. Complete stage settings were built in Cleveland, a local chorus of up to eighty voices was used, and comprimario parts were assigned to local artists." Among the operas presented was *Lady Macbeth of Mzensk* by Shostakovitch, which was later performed by this organization at the Metropolitan Opera House as well as at the Academy of Music in Philadelphia.

Even before these experiments with opera as part of the regular concert series, Leopold Stokowski had achieved memorable operatic performances with the Philadelphia Orchestra. Among them were Schönberg's *Glückliche Hand* and *Pierrot Lunaire*, Strawinsky's *Oedipus Rex* and the American première of Alban Berg's *Wozzeck*.

Later, in 1945, Max Reiter founded the annual Opera Festival of the San Antonio Symphony Orchestra. Continued under Victor Alessandro, this Festival has become an eagerly-awaited event in Texas. Four operas are performed each spring. The manager of the Symphony Society of San Antonio, Clinton E. Norton, states: "Our operas are underwritten by guarantors in the amount of $500 each. We usually have approximately thirty underwriters, and in our entire history we have had to call upon them only once." For several years since 1952, Karl Schwieger, the conductor of the Kansas City Symphony has given two operas in staged form during the last two weeks of the symphony season.

Opera has appeared to an increasing extent in the repertory of symphony orchestras throughout the country. One reason for this may be the fact that a majority of the symphony conductors have been Europeans who formerly were closely connected with operatic activities. Arturo Toscanini, Bruno Walter, Fritz Reiner, Georg Szell, William Steinberg, Maurice Abravanel, Max Rudolf, Karl Krips and others held leading positions in European opera houses. Dimitri Mitropoulos, Erich Leinsdorf, Karl Schwieger, Laszlo Halasz and many more started as coaches in opera houses. It is not surprising that they were sympathetic to the presentation of opera, at least in concert form, when they became conductors of American symphony orchestras.

Bruno Walter conducted Gluck's *Orfeo* in concert form in the New York Philharmonic series as long ago as 1935. Mitropoulos conducted several concert versions of operas at the Stadium Concerts in New York City before he presented works like Strauss' *Elektra*, Busoni's *Arlecchino* and Alban Berg's *Wozzeck* as part of the regular Philharmonic series. The series of operas which Toscanini conducted on nationwide radio broadcasts during his tenure as Musical Director of the NBC Orchestra gave particular impetus to the presentation of opera in concert form. At the same time, largely spurred by these activities and by the increasing availability of operatic recordings, the American public showed ever increasing enthusiasm for opera.

Need for collaboration

With the establishment of community opera, it has become obvious that the potential co-operation between symphony orchestras and operatic groups ought to be exploited to the full. The symphony orchestras, on the one hand, are striving for wider support and more extended seasons. Community opera, on the other hand, is in desperate need of a professional orchestra as the first requisite for operation. The stage is set for some kind of collaboration, despite formidable obstacles which are in part the outgrowth of American tradition.

In the United States the symphony orchestra came into being before opera, and independently of opera. Major American cities have long since accepted the obligation of supporting their symphony orchestras, and as a result practically every large city has an orchestra of very high quality. Civic opera, on the other hand, is a comparative newcomer on the American scene. Though growing, it is not yet recognized as a cultural obligation to the same extent. In Europe, of course, this process was reversed; opera houses were established first, and later the opera orchestras gave concerts as well. Opera conductors and many opera composers grew up in the orchestra pits of the opera houses. Today in most European cities, opera and symphony orchestras are identical. America, relying on private subsidy, may well discover that it is impractical to support symphony orchestras in their traditional splendid isolation from opera.

Present developments indicate new trends. Characteristically, a leading musical magazine, *Musical America*, has published a series of editorials entitled "Operation

Symphony-Opera USA," advocating collaboration between the two institutions.* The editors stated: "The time has come, we believe, for our orchestras to recognize the obvious fact that the symphony orchestra and opera are natural allies, and that both stand to achieve impressive gains by making common cause together."

Successful examples

Replying to inquiries by *Musical America*, various orchestral organizations have reported overwhelming success in their operatic presentations. These organizations included symphony orchestras presenting opera in concert form, such as the Seattle Symphony, the Tri-City Symphony in Davenport, Iowa, and the orchestras in Toledo and Grand Rapids, among many others; and also those presenting full-scale stage productions of opera, such as the Buffalo Symphony and the Washington National Symphony, which presented both opera and ballet. There were also orchestras which are progressing from concert performances to semi-staged and finally to full-fledged opera productions. The Duluth Symphony, for example, began by presenting six operas in concert form using imported singers. *Musical America* quoted the manager, A. H. Miller, as follows: "We started giving these operas with some fear and trepidation, wondering how opera would go here in Duluth; but, to our surprise, they were all received most enthusiastically. We have made them an annual presentation. Now that they have met with such success here, indicating a keen interest in opera, we are toying with the idea of presenting grand opera with scenery and costumes, although we have been doing our concert form opera with costumes and a spattering of stage props to help emphasize the action of the story. With us, as with many others, performances of opera have furnished a new facet for attracting more and more people to our concerts and also serving a dual purpose in giving opera and symphony to our audiences."

The musical director of the Cedar Rapids Symphony, Henry Denecke, reports after putting on his first concert performance of an opera, *Traviata:* "This is our first opera, but already so much enthusiasm is evinced that I'm planning *Fledermaus* with scenery and costumes for next year. In order to produce this I have suggested that the Art Association and Community Theater also collaborate, the former for the scenery and the latter for direction. This is an ideal

* *Musical America*, December, 1957; January and March, 1958.

solution because all three groups then serve the community in the united effort. The Cedar Rapids Civic Chorus also will take part. This group I formed three years ago so that we could do the Beethoven Ninth, and have used every year since."

More symphony orchestras present opera

It is evident that in many American cities symphony and opera are beginning to understand their common interest. The list of symphonic organizations presenting opera is growing constantly. At the Central Opera Service Conference of 1958, Helen M. Thompson of the American Symphony League reported that during the season of 1955–56 eighteen symphony organizations gave operas. Fourteen of the productions were concert presentations, and four were staged. Only two seasons later, in 1957–58, forty-one orchestras produced a total of forty-nine operas. Of these, ten were staged and thirty-nine done in concert form. By 1959, the number of symphony orchestras which presented opera regularly in concert form had risen to forty-eight. And this list includes only operas presented as part of the concert season. It does not include such added enterprises as the annual Opera Festival of the San Antonio Symphony Orchestra, or the summer opera productions at Salt Lake City. Some of these orchestras specialize in concert or semi-staged performances of little-known operas. Two such organizations are the Little Orchestra Society and the New York Opera Society.

The production of opera by the local symphony itself is, of course, not the only way in which opera can be linked to the local orchestra. In many cases the operatic group engages members of the local symphony on an individual basis to form its own opera orchestra. In other communities official collaboration between the opera-producing company and the symphony can be achieved. This works out to the benefit of both. For example, in Salt Lake City collaboration between the University and the Symphony means, according to Abravanel, "that the twenty-week season of our seventy musicians on full contract (we use seventy to ninety-six according to the works performed) is extended to twenty-two weeks for fifty-five musicians and twenty-seven and one-half for our top thirty-five players. We have a long way to go, but I think that eventually we will have an almost year-round operation in Utah, including opera, ballet and symphony."

In Houston an interesting agreement has been reached between the managements

96

of the Opera and the Symphony. During its first three seasons the Opera Company formed its orchestra by engaging individual members of the Houston Symphony. Later, however, the two organizations signed a contract under which the Symphony Orchestra was to be employed for three full weeks during the 1959–1962 opera seasons, with forty-eight hours of rehearsals and nine performances each season. The agreement stipulated payments of $20,000 for the first, $22,500 for the second, and $25,000 for the third season. This was designed not only to extend the regular contracts of the players by one week; it would also contribute to a pension fund for the orchestra. Furthermore, due to the fact that three weeks of the Symphony were now to belong officially to the Opera Company, it was expected that the musical public would no longer be split into two competing factions. The two regular opera performances were planned for Monday and Tuesday evenings, which are normally the evenings for symphony concerts. Both symphony and opera would be presented in the same hall. Thus an important step was taken in Houston towards collaboration, if not actual integration, between symphony orchestra and community opera.

Financial Support

The American way of opera organization

In contrast to direct government subsidy of opera in Europe, America is developing its own methods of community sponsorship based on its own social and economic traditions. This sponsorship takes various forms, but the first and most important one is support by private individuals.

In America an opera company is usually set up as a corporate entity operating under a board of directors or governors. This board is made up of prominent civic leaders and businessmen and is led by a group of officers—normally a president, vice-president, secretary and treasurer. It appoints the administration, which conducts the artistic and business operation of the company.

The opera association is supported by committees. These include the executive committee, the women's boards and so forth. Frequently additional support is guaranteed by sustaining members, sponsors and patrons; corporations and business firms often make substantial contributions. Under certain arrangements these individuals agree to underwrite operating losses up to a certain amount.

The opera guild

Of particular importance to any community opera is the local opera guild. This type of organization is usually modeled after the Metropolitan Opera Guild, which has become the backbone of democratic support for opera. Through membership and executive activities the opera guilds help stimulate interest in opera and solicit contributions. They assist in the organization of school performances, in raising funds for new productions, in finding support for young singers. There are also various other forms of guilds and committees: women's guilds, junior committees, student councils, etc.

Student performances In 1960 the Metropolitan Opera Guild contributed about $100,000 to the Metropolitan Opera Association and sponsored seven student performances of *Don Giovanni* for 23,000 school children from the New York area. In collaboration with the New York Board of Regents, the Guild participated in a new educational television project designed to bring understanding of opera to 100,000 children in schoolrooms throughout Greater New York.

National Council Again under the guidance of Mrs. Belmont, the Metropolitan Opera founded the National Council in 1952 to promote "nationwide participation in the development of the Metropolitan as a national institution." Among the tasks of the National Council was the establishment of the Central Opera Service, which was founded to promote "the development of opera of high artistic standards among university workshops, civic and professional companies, music camps, 'grass roots' and television groups."

Central Opera Service Organized in 1954, the Central Opera Service has proved to be a valuable center for contact and exchange of information between the numerous operatic groups in the country. The annual spring conferences of this organization have been outstanding events. On these occasions members and delegates from some 100 opera-producing organizations throughout the nation exchange ideas and gain information. The Spring Conference of 1960 was a co-operative undertaking sponsored jointly by the Central Opera Service and the National Association for Opera. The latter group is devoted to the same goal of assisting American operatic production in all its aspects. The Central Opera Service also publishes an *Opera Manual*, which offers detailed information concerning operatic production.

The National Council sponsors one new production each year for the Metropolitan. It has also organized the Regional Auditions Program and holds auditions for young singers in eleven centrally-located cities throughout the nation. Regional winners are given an audition on the Metropolitan stage. The final winners receive awards ranging from a Metropolitan contract to scholarships for operatic training.

Entire new productions of opera at the Metropolitan Opera and the Lyric Opera of Chicago have been made possible by contributions from either individuals or foundations, which more recently have become actively interested in supporting opera. The Rockefeller Foundation made a grant of $200,000 to the New York City Center, over the three-year period 1953–55, for the commissioning of new productions in the fields of ballet and opera. In 1958, the Ford Foundation gave the New York City Center Opera a grant of $105,000 to produce a spring season of ten American operas. This sum covered 40 per cent of the budget for the five-week season, with an additional $5,000 to pay the expenses of composers attending rehearsals. The remaining 60 per cent was contributed by the New York City Center of Music and Drama. We mentioned earlier that the Ford Foundation followed this contribution with another grant of $310,000 for the subsequent two seasons of American opera.

In 1953, the Rockefeller Foundation gave $400,000 to the Louisville Philharmonic Society for the commissioning and presentation of modern music, including two new operas annually for four years. This grant was, in successive years, augmented by $100,000. In 1957, the Ford Foundation offered a grant of $165,000 to the Experimental Opera Theatre of America, a training center affiliated with the New Orleans Opera House Association directed by Renato Cellini, to put on three five-week seasons of operatic performances with young American singers over a three-year period. These seasons follow the regular spring seasons of the Opera House Association. By the end of 1959, E.O.T.A. had produced seventeen different operas in some forty performances and given many young singers a springboard for activity in the United States as well as in Europe.

In 1959, the Ford Foundation announced a grant of $950,000 to the Metropolitan Opera, Chicago Lyric Opera, San Francisco and New York City Opera Companies, for the presentation of eighteen new operas to be written by Americans. And the most generous support ever made to the cause of opera were grants in millions of dollars by both the Rockefeller and Ford Foundations towards the creation of the new Lincoln Center for the Performing Arts in New York City, which of course includes opera in its program, as well as training for careers in opera.

In the United States the system of private sponsorship by individuals and foundations is developing a network of new approaches to democratic support of opera. Nothing like this exists in Europe. There are also various funds which provide scholarships for young operatic artists. Among these are the Fulbright Program and the Baird-Rockefeller Aid to Music Program. These funds enable young singers and directors to complete their studies and possibly find engagements in Europe.

Commercial sponsorship

In addition to the private sponsorship we have mentioned, American opera companies may receive revenue from commercial sources. The financial statements of the Metropolitan Opera, for instance, show income from radio and television, recording fees and building rentals. These activities bring in more than $500,000 each year. The New York City Center, by renting its theatre to profitable theatrical enterprises, renting its studios, etc., manages to reduce its operating deficit substantially. Television and film will provide major sources of income when opera appears more often on these media.

Government support

There are also important instances of government support of opera, however. We have noted the contributions made by the City of San Francisco to its opera company, and the subsidy furnished by the Los Angeles County Board of Supervisors to the Guild Opera Company. Other cities provide support in a different but very significant way. New York City puts a municipally-owned theatre at the disposal of the New York City Center, Inc., for a token fee. Kansas City made available the Civic Auditorium to its orchestra without cost, and the orchestra has in the past produced several operas.

In the concert field a precedent has been set in Minneapolis. Here the University of Minnesota gives its Northrop Auditorium to the Symphony Orchestra for a modest charge, which the University returns to the Orchestra by purchasing tickets for students. There is little doubt that this arrangement could be extended to include opera produced in collaboration with the Symphony.

Perhaps these instances of taxpayers' money being used for operatic purposes do not seem very significant in the total picture, yet we should take notice that they do exist and undoubtedly could be multiplied. Two avenues of approach seem immediately promising: (1) free use of a building owned by a city or university; and (2) financial assistance to the opera in return for student tickets. It cannot be denied that reliance on private support and commercial income involves a certain instability. Not only can the economic fortune of the sponsors vary a great deal from time to time, but there is the continuing worry of raising a considerable sum annually. For these reasons, the establishment of endowment funds is obviously desirable in order to make possible long-range planning. It may not be possible to organize such funds immediately in every city. But in a few communities another form of sponsorship of great significance has already become a reality: the United Arts Fund. In most cities the local symphony, the opera company, the arts institutions and other cultural enterprises conduct separate fund-raising campaigns. This usually means a division of the community into groups, and even factions, backing individual cultural enterprises. The cities of Cincinnati and Louisville recognized this problem and decided to do something about it. They accordingly organized an annual United Arts Fund Drive, patterned on the idea of the Community Chest. This type of campaign has proved beneficial for each of the individual arts as well as for the arts as a whole. For while not every citizen may be interested in supporting the symphony, the opera or the fine arts as such, most will agree that it is necessary and desirable to support culture in general.

United community sponsorship

In 1949 the first United Arts Fund was organized in Cincinnati by the Cincinnati Institute of Fine Arts. The background of this institution will be of interest to other communities, and I am grateful to Mr. Leslie C. White, Manager of the Institute, for the following information:

Cincinnati's United Arts Fund

"The Cincinnati Institute of Fine Arts was organized in 1927 for the purpose of underwriting operational expenses for Cincinnati's cultural institutions. An original endowment of $3,500,000 was collected through a capital funds drive.

"The organization of the Institute was primarily inspired by the desire of Mr. and Mrs. Charles P. Taft to guarantee continuing support for the Cincinnati Symphony Orchestra. Mr. and Mrs. Taft agreed to give $1,000,000 to a non-profit civic organization provided a matching $2,500,000 was raised from the public. The Cincinnati Institute of Fine Arts was organized to raise and administer the endowment."

Despite an additional contribution by the original sponsors, the Depression and World War II made it impossible to give sufficient support to the city's cultural organization through this endowment alone. "Therefore, in 1949," Mr. White continues, "with the individual organizations finding it more and more impossible to make ends meet, the United Fine Arts Fund was organized as this country's first Community Chest-like campaign for the arts."

The first campaign raised nearly $100,000 more than drives by individual organizations had been able to accomplish. Since that time the base of contributors has been broadened from an original 3,500 to 17,500 in 1959, and the money raised has been increased from more than $250,000 in 1949 to $354,500 in 1959. Of this amount $66,900 was allotted in 1959 to the Cincinnati Summer Opera Association. The 1960 goal of $375,850 was to be distributed by the Institute of Fine Arts, which administers the Fund, to the following institutions in these amounts: Cincinnati Symphony Orchestra, $148,500; Cincinnati Art Museum, $81,600; Taft Museum, $29,850; Cincinnati Summer Opera, $87,900; and the rest, $28,000, will be used to cover administration and campaign expenses.

"The Summer Opera's total budget in 1960," Mr. White explains, "was approximately $225,000. You might be interested to know that the 1960 allotment to the Summer Opera represents an increase of $26,000 over 1958, an increase of nearly 43 per cent. We feel that this is a good answer to the often-heard argument that united funds tend to hold back artistic improvement in individual operations. In 1959 and again in 1960 our opera staging has been completely refurbished, primarily through increased allotments from the United Fine Arts Fund."

The Louisville Fund   In a similar way the city of Louisville, Kentucky, under the forward-looking Mayor Charles P. Farnsley, instituted the Louisville Fund, after having expanded its remarkable system of public libraries as a center for the dissemination of the arts through books, FM broadcasting, recordings and films. The Louisville Fund is an annual Community Chest of the arts which serves the following institutions: the Louisville Orchestra, the Art Center Association, the Kentucky Opera Association, a Junior Art Gallery, the Louisville Dance Council and a Children's Theater. In the year 1957 the Fund campaigned for $125,000. Eighty per cent of this amount was obtained in the form of "special gifts," the rest by person-to-person collections. A board governs the Fund and determines the appropriations. The secretary of the Orchestra is also the secretary of the Fund. Moritz Bomhard, Director of the Opera Association, comments: "We continue to be a member of the Louisville Fund. Almost every year since our beginning our

102

appropriation has been raised. All of our deficit is being covered from this source."

Since the Fund serves a variety of cultural purposes, it is considered an essential civic undertaking which benefits every family. This cultural support has also proved very practical. A representative of General Electric, for instance, stated that the city's concern with cultural activities strongly influenced his company in its decision to transfer a major plant to Louisville—a move involving 700 to 800 families. J. R. Poteat of General Electric, in a speech delivered at a Special Gifts Luncheon for the Louisville Fund on January 18, 1956, asked rhetorically: "So why should Louisville business and industry be interested in the Louisville Fund? . . . This Fund is fostering institutions in which the children of the community can develop many talents, and this makes for happy and creative family life. It is giving Louisville people many areas in which tensions of modern living can be relieved by participation in creative arts."

Cincinnati's United Fine Arts Fund and the Louisville Fund have set significant examples for the rest of the country, and have shown how the American community can undertake sponsorship of the arts, including opera.

2. THE OPERA THEATRE

Treasured old opera houses

It is not surprising that America, lacking the strong European historic and social concern with opera, has not yet found a characteristic architectural solution for the presentation of this art form. In America there are, on the one hand, treasured old opera theatres like the Metropolitan Opera House in New York and the Academy of Music in Philadelphia. These are fine imitations of European originals. Or we find more democratic structures dating from the period following World War I, such as the Civic Opera House of Chicago and the War Memorial Opera House in San Francisco. In contrast, there are quaint old opera houses like the one in Central City, Colorado, dating from Gold Rush days.

But there are few examples of an original approach to opera house design comparable to the creative ideas pioneered by American architects in other fields. An exception would be the old Auditorium in Chicago, created by the father of American architecture, Louis Sullivan. This building, although today in a dilapidated state, still awakens the admiration of the visitor because of its fine proportions, its excellent sightlines, the arrangement of the boxes, the free, overhanging balcony and the ascending ceiling, to say nothing of the excellent acoustics which seasoned Chicago opera lovers remember with nostalgia.

New Orleans and Boston, traditional centers of Grand Opera, have lost their historic opera houses and have no proper home for opera today. The situation is the same in most other American cities, where opera has to be accommodated in commercial theatres, auditoriums, concert halls or movie houses, if there is no university theatre available. The unstable status of opera in America is reflected in the fact that no opera company, except for the Metropolitan, owns its own house.

Not a single new professional opera house has been built in the United States during the past quarter of a century, with the exception of the small outdoor theatre in Santa Fé, New Mexico. Stage layout and stage equipment in existing opera houses are for the most part hopelessly outdated. In Europe, because of the shift from painted perspective backdrops to three-dimensional scenery, the relationship between auditorium and stage has changed from 1:1 to 1:2, or even 1:3. America's opera houses still preserve the 1:1 proportions of opera's oil-and-candle-lamp days. With the exception of the San Francisco and Chicago opera houses, there is no adequate modern technical equipment. There are no sliding and elevator stages, no up-to-date lighting equipment; nor do we find sufficient workroom and storage areas. In all of today's major American opera theatres, the proscenium remains an inflexible picture frame.

Progressive American projects; Norman Bel Geddes

All of this seems odd, since American designers and architects have long since conceived projects for the legitimate theatre more progressive than anything to be found in Europe. As early as 1922, Norman Bel Geddes advocated in plans and articles a stage freed from the limitations of the proscenium. That was five years before Gropius advanced his project of the "Totaltheater" in Europe, and eleven years before the arena stage at the Realistic Theatre in Moscow.

First theatres in-the-round

In 1932 the School of Drama at the University of Washington put on the first production of a play in-the-round, in a drawing room of a penthouse atop Seattle's Edmond Meany Hotel. The School continued this type of production successfully during the following eight years, in various other quarters, until in 1950 a permanent theatre was built on the campus by the Director, Glenn

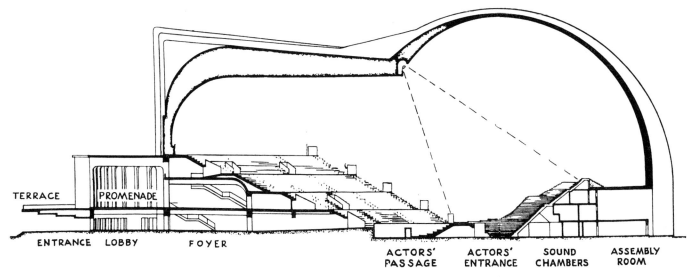

61 An American pioneer's project: Norman Bel Geddes' plan for a "Divine Comedy Theater" (1929)

Hughes, based on preliminary plans by John Ashby Conway, Art Director. The University of Washington Theatre was the first of its kind.

Other theatres in-the-round soon followed, such as the one at the University of Miami. At Dallas, in 1947, Margo Jones opened the first professional theatre for plays presented in-the-round. Since 1949, Benno Frank has produced operas at Karamu's arena theatre in Cleveland on a regular basis. The idea of a stage in the center of the audience, which in Europe has been adopted only for the Teatro Sant'Erasmo in Milan and as one possible arrangement of Mannheim's smaller house, was accepted enthusiastically in America. Summer tent theatres sprang up throughout the country. In these, light opera and occasionally Grand Opera are presented, as at Cleveland's Musicarnival tent theatre. Such experiments prove that there are other ways to produce musical theatre which are quite as effective as the traditional peephole proscenium method, with the audience kept at a distance from the play.

Flexible theatres   Yet, obviously, the rigidity of the old proscenium theatre is paralleled by the inflexibility of the usual theatre in-the-round. Designers asked themselves whether it was not possible to create a theatre which would permit both types of production. Attempts have been made in Europe to achieve greater flexibility within the proscenium area, as in the theatres of Malmö, Bochum, Augsburg and Salzburg, but it was again an American, Norman Bel Geddes, who first broke with traditional approaches. In an article entitled, "Towards A More Flexible Theatre,"* Bel Geddes made the following radical proposal to educational institutions:

"The present-day proscenium theatre is the most limiting form of structure the theatre has ever known. My plea is for a new type of theatre, a theatre which will permit other than proscenium type productions. This does not rule out the proscenium type production . . . Another limitation of the present theatre is the elaborate and cumbersome mechanical stage system. All of our ideas pertaining to handling of scenery on the stage have been derived from Germany. There, prior to the first World War, the Germans developed mechanical stage techniques to the highest point yet achieved. The results were wonderful for what they sought to accomplish, but they are elaborate and unnecessary for the theatre I am discussing. Elevating stages, revolving stages, pivot stages, sliding stages, permanent cycloramas, double proscenium arches, all are unnecessary to good theatre. They impose limitations on every production on that stage."

In 1949, Frank Lloyd Wright presented a *Project for a New Theatre* at Hartford, Connecticut, "designed to free the so-called legitimate stage from its peep-show character and high stagehouse overhead, establishing a simple workable basis for presenting plays as a circumstance in the round. Now the show is more like a painting; a scene-drop behind a proscenium frame—audience in one room, performers in another. In the New Theatre audience and performers are under one ceiling—almost in one room—more like sculpture."**

An innovator of theatre technique: George C. Izenour

The idea of the flexible theatre has been seconded by another great American, the designer-engineer George C. Izenour. I visited his office and laboratory at Yale University and listened to his explanations of a new theatre project for Carnegie Institute of Technology at Pittsburgh. He declared, "I am not simply against the proscenium theatre, because we cannot disregard the works conceived for this traditional form of theatre, and those we cannot and should not perform without that device. But I don't see why we should force our present

* Printed and distributed by the Dramatist's Play Service, New York City.

** This project was never realized, but Mr. Wright's ideas eventually found expression in the Dallas Theater Center (see illustrations 76–79).

or future authors to be bound by it. Therefore, I think, we must have a theatre which makes all types of production possible."

With this sensible approach Izenour, the master theoretician of the modern space theatre, went on to explain his model for the experimental theatre at Yale. Here I felt that great uncompromising American idealism which, as in the work of Bel Geddes and Robert Edmond Jones, speaks without undue weight of tradition and with the conviction of truth. Why should there be any limitation of fantasy in theatre production, either with regard to the proscenium or the convention of scenery hung in lines parallel to the footlights? Why should there not be action and scenery at any point in the theatrical space, and in any relation to the audience? This thinking resulted in four types of flexibility: (1) a new floor, combining auditorium and stage; (2) a new grid overhanging both; (3) a new approach to lighting equipment; and (4) a correspondingly new system of automatic controls.

As can be seen in the illustration 72, the rectangular floor is divided into forty-five eight-foot-square sections. This area is five sections wide and nine sections long. Each of these square sections is mounted on a hydraulic piston having an eleven-foot stroke. Twenty of the eight-foot-square sections contain two smaller segment platforms, four-by-eight feet in size, also mounted on pistons. The remaining twenty-five sections are made up of four two-by-eight-foot segment platforms mounted on individual pistons. The stroke of these segment pistons is two feet, six inches each. The combined stroke of the segment pistons plus the section pistons provides a total travel of thirteen feet, six inches in the vertical plane. The illustration (Number 74) shows a view with the audience at one end and the stage at the other. The other illustration (Number 75) shows the audience seated on three sides of the acting area.

The flexibility of the floor is paralleled by that of the ceiling overhanging it; "a channel-type gridiron structure which is eighteen feet above the main peripheral level of the floor. From this grid movable screens are suspended. The gridiron is scaled the same as the floor and consists of two-foot squares, which, when repeated, form the tracks in which the scenery carriages move. Since the individual channel boxes are square, movement of the scenery is effected longitudinally and transversely throughout the entire grid mesh."

Again, corresponding with this flexible system of floor and ceiling, the lighting system permits the placement and movement of lamps at or to any point above or below the grid. These are all controlled by Izenour's electronic switchboard.* The lighting system operates automatically. But even more revolutionary is the fact that all the technical equipment of the theatre is masterminded by a single central control system using a "common storage memory and scanning amplifier system for the floor and lighting systems."

As a logical consequence of his endeavor to control any point within the stage space, Izenour has replaced the traditional grid system of "sets of lines," which permit the hanging of scenery primarily only parallel to the footlights, by a new system of single lines. These run on winches mounted above the grid, over movable sheaves, and descend from any point down through the grid. They are controlled electronically, either individually or synchronously in groups, by an operator who sits on a movable console on the stage. The console contains presets and governs grouping of the winches, run and speed. This "electronically controlled synchronous winch system" was first installed at Hofstra College, Hempstead, L.I., in 1959.

Now the first of Izenour's theatres, the Loeb Drama Center of Harvard University at Cambridge, Massachusetts, is under construction. According to Hugh Stubbins, the architect, Harvard had requested that "the stage be adaptable enough to accommodate any classical or modern play and to present it in a manner consistent with the style in which it is written . . . Briefly, the solution was attained by keeping that portion of the seating back of the cross-aisle permanent and inclined, and that portion of the seating in front of the cross-aisle closest to the stage, flexible, mechanized and on lifts. The plan includes a device by which thirteen tons of seating can be moved in thirty minutes. The first 140 seats are on motorized platforms and can be shifted to the right and left sides. The stage, also on lifts, is converted into various shapes and levels."**

Izenour acted as consultant for the Harvard Theatre and engineered the flexible arrangement, as well as the lighting and stage machinery. The theatre at the Carnegie Institute of Technology will be realized next. These are Izenour's answers to the skeptical opposition of the so-called "practical" men in the

* Manufactured and distributed by the Twentieth Century Lighting Company.
** Hugh Stubbins, "University Drama Center," *Architectural Record*, October, 1959.

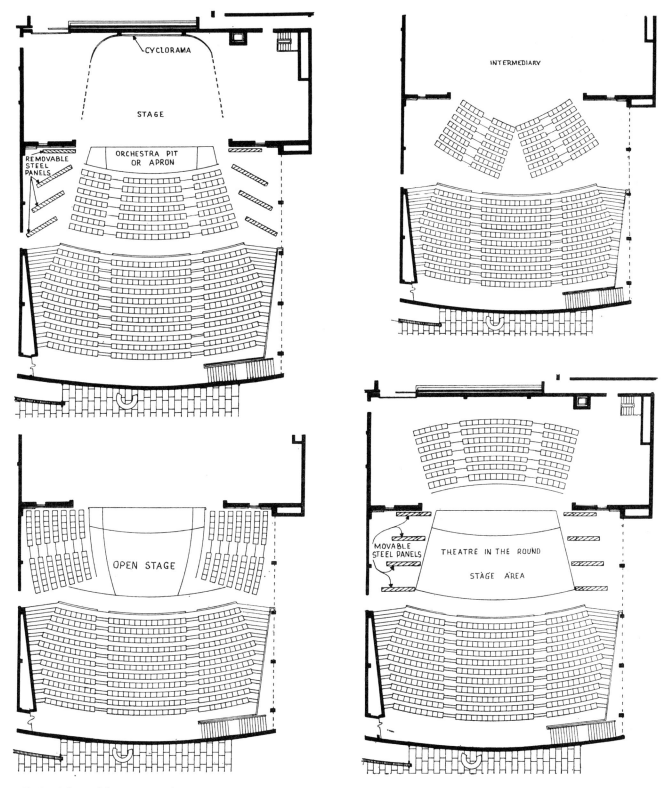

CYCLORAMA

STAGE

ORCHESTRA PIT
OR APRON

REMOVABLE
STEEL
PANELS

INTERMEDIARY

OPEN STAGE

MOVABLE
STEEL
PANELS

THEATRE IN THE ROUND

STAGE AREA

62–65 The multi-purpose Loeb Drama Center at Harvard University, Cambridge, Mass. (1960); Hugh Stubbins, architect, and George C. Izenour, technical engineer. (These four groundplans illustrate the flexibility of the theatre, ranging from proscenium stage to theatre in-the-round.)

theatre, who will be forgotten just as certainly as Izenour's ideas will be used in practice and his name remembered as a pioneer of American theatre technique.

Other modern stage technicians In addition to new concepts of theatre in-the-round and flexible staging, America has developed new technical devices. In the field of lighting, Izenour's magnetic amplifier switchboard finds competition from another type constructed by the Metropolitan Electric Manufacturing Company. New projection equipment has been invented under the stimulus of television and movies. The "Cinerama" cyclorama has shown the audience what it is like to be engulfed in action. Lighting experts like Abe Feder, who has also been busy promoting a multi-purpose stage, Jean Rosenthal and others have specialized in new lighting techniques. Audio engineers like the firm of Bolt, Beranek and Newman, Inc., as well as others, are penetrating into the mysteries of frequently elusive acoustics; while Ben Schlanger concentrates on the problems of good sightlines in theatres and concert halls. Long before stereophonic sound added an acoustical third dimension to records and films, Harold Burris-Meyer and others* were writing books about electronic control of sound in the theatre and experimenting in this field.

New school theatres While uncompromising minds like Bel Geddes and Izenour worked out new theories of stage design in its purest form, practical theatre construction finally began to get under way, guided by a new spirit, after many years of inertia. For some time Lee Simonson had been proposing theatres for schools. In 1953 Marcel Breuer built a theatre for Sarah Lawrence College at Bronxville, N.Y. In 1956, Denison University of Granville, Ohio, dedicated its Theatre Arts Building. This theatre, built in 1956 and designed by William Gehron with Edward Cole of Yale as consultant, is a multi-purpose design of simple and yet efficient type.

New theatres in Canada Across the border in Canada the Shakespeare Festival at Stratford, Ontario, gradually improved its original tent theatre, which had been built with assistance from the Rockefeller Foundation and was a unique adaption of the Elizabethan theatre. In 1957, with the help of remarkable donations from the Canadian government and from private sources, this canvas tent was replaced

---

* Harold Burris-Meyer and Vincent Mallory, *Sound in the Theatre* (Mineola, New York: Radio Magazines, Inc., 1959).

110

by an excellent modern building. Because it followed the form of the Elizabethan theatre this house has succeeded in accommodating an audience of 2,190, with no seat more than sixty-five feet from the stage. The Vancouver Festival, also in Canada, was started in 1958. By the following year it had erected a $6,000,000 theatre seating 2,800. A second theatre seating 700 was scheduled to open the following year.

New theatres and arts centers in the United States

In the United States a similar movement has begun to unfold. First, Stratford, Connecticut, opened its own Shakespearean Theatre. In 1958, an Arts Center Theatre was built in Boston, with a stage adaptable for either proscenium or three-quarter-round production. At Los Angeles, Welton Becket and Associates are planning a new Music Center incorporating a theatre able to accommodate symphony, opera and light opera.

At Dallas the only theatre project of Frank Lloyd Wright that was to become a reality opened in December, 1959, eight months after the death of the famous architect. The Dallas Theatre Center has no proscenium. The stage has a total frontage of seventy feet. A central area contains a thirty-two-foot revolving table which protrudes into the audience. There are two side stages.

In New York, The Lincoln Center for the Performing Arts is well along on its grandiose scheme to create for the first time an entire cultural complex, combining opera house, symphony hall, ballet theatre, legitimate playhouse, music school and museum-library. Theatre architects who had been inactive for a quarter of a century, ever since the construction of Radio City and its Center Theatre Opera House, suddenly found themselves embroiled in feverish activity. Among those working there are Wallace K. Harrison, Max Abramowitz, Philip Johnson, Pietro Belluschi, Eero Saarinen and Joe Mielziner, who for some time has been enthusiastically proposing a theatre with a flexible proscenium.

In Washington, D.C., the government appropriated a site for a National Cultural Center. Plans have been drawn up by Edward Durell Stone, who, with Donald Oenslager, was responsible for the American Theatre at the Brussels World's Fair. Stone is being assisted by an advisory committee which includes Donald Oenslager, Ben Schlanger, Walther Unruh and myself. He proposes a Pantheon-like cupola embracing three main buildings and two smaller auditoriums in one imposing edifice facing the Potomac River. If this is carried through, the nation will achieve here a setting worthy of its cultural gifts.

Now theatre plans are being discussed in practically every city. Realizing the importance of the new projects, the Ford Foundation has sponsored a program to develop new ideas on theatre planning through teams of designers. Indicative of the new trend is the fact that the recipients of grants include such men as George C. Izenour, Frederick J. Kiesler, Joe Mielziner and Ben Schlanger, who are all designing convertible types of theatres.

ANTA's advising agency

In order to set professional standards, the American National Theatre and Academy has organized a "Board of Standards and Planning for the Living Theatre." The leading American architects and theatrical experts on the Board are joining forces to guide those who seek advice in designing new theatre projects for American communities.

Need for multi-purpose theatres

How should new theatres be designed to accommodate opera in America? Obviously, planners must take realistic account of the facts opera faces. Very few cities can hope to build and operate a theatre solely for the purpose of opera production. In smaller cities the theatre must serve for public meetings and other functions; and opera will probably have to share the theatre with the symphony, the light opera, the ballet and the spoken play. In the past, relatively few American concert halls were built primarily for symphony concerts. Among the few are the symphony halls in Boston, Chicago and Cleveland, and the fine Kleinhans Concert Hall by Saarinen at Buffalo. Normally, even if the orchestra group owns the building, it shares it with the opera, as in Philadelphia, Kansas City, San Francisco, Denver, Houston, etc. Another practical consideration is television. Economic necessity and civic interest will indoubtedly require telecasts of actual performances from the new theatres, and this again imposes certain technical considerations. Thus it seems certain that the future American theatre will have to have greater flexibility and simpler technical equipment than that found in the typical European opera house.

Since conditions in America are in every way quite different from those of Europe, it is only logical that direct imitation of European opera theatres will not provide the answer for America. While accepting judiciously the best applicable features of European engineering artistry and experience, the American theatre designer should leave the door open to the vigorous new ideas created here at home. These, unhampered by tradition, go beyond the great European achievements and point toward the future.

112

Two treasured old American
opera houses.

66 The Metropolitan Opera
    House in New York
    (1883), an imitation of
    Europe's great
    opera houses.

67 The old Auditorium at
    Chicago. Built by Louis
    Sullivan, this theatre
    represented an original
    approach by that great
    American architect.

68 The Red Rocks Theatre near Denver, Colorado; Burnham Hoyt, architect.

69 Musical theatre in-the-round: The Musicarnival Tent at Cleveland, Ohio.

70 The Sarah Lawrence
Art Center at
Bronxville,
New York (1953);
Marcel Breuer,
architect.

71 The American
Theatre
at the Brussels
World's Fair, 1958.
Edward Durell
Stone was the
architect and
Donald Oenslager
acted as stage
consultant for this
project.

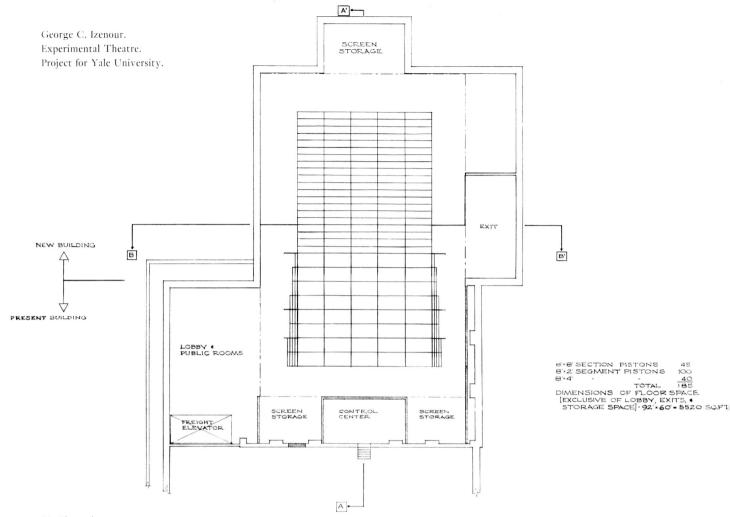

George C. Izenour.
Experimental Theatre.
Project for Yale University.

NEW BUILDING

PRESENT BUILDING

SCREEN STORAGE

EXIT

LOBBY & PUBLIC ROOMS

FREIGHT ELEVATOR

SCREEN STORAGE

CONTROL CENTER

SCREEN STORAGE

8'×8' SECTION PISTONS   45
8'×2' SEGMENT PISTONS   100
8'×4'   "   40
      TOTAL   185
DIMENSIONS OF FLOOR SPACE
[EXCLUSIVE OF LOBBY, EXITS, &
STORAGE SPACE]·92'×60'=5520 SQ.FT

72 Floor plan.

73 Longitudinal section.

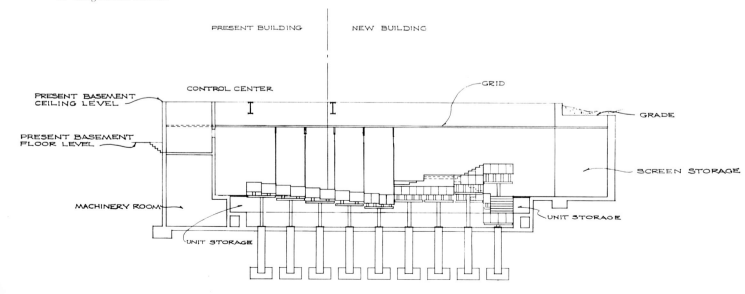

PRESENT BUILDING   NEW BUILDING

CONTROL CENTER   GRID

PRESENT BASEMENT CEILING LEVEL

GRADE

PRESENT BASEMENT FLOOR LEVEL

SCREEN STORAGE

MACHINERY ROOM

UNIT STORAGE

UNIT STORAGE

74 Drawing showing audience seated on one side of the acting area.

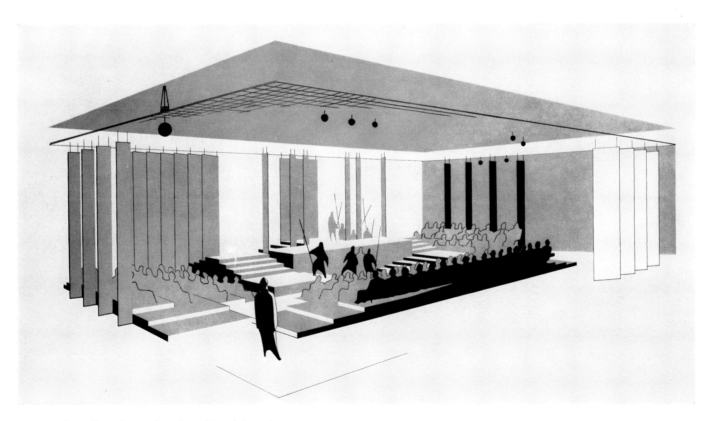

75 Here the audience is seated on three sides of the acting area.

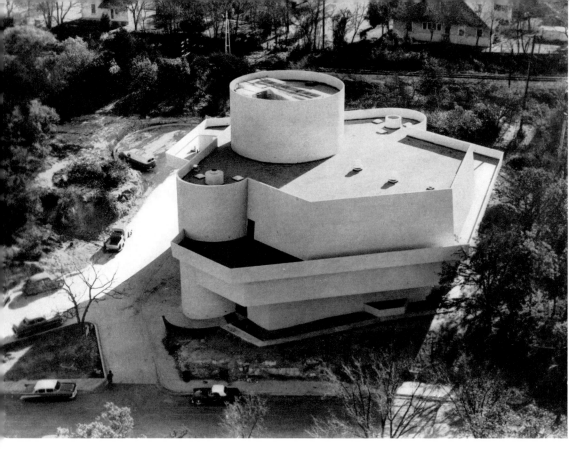

76 Exterior view.

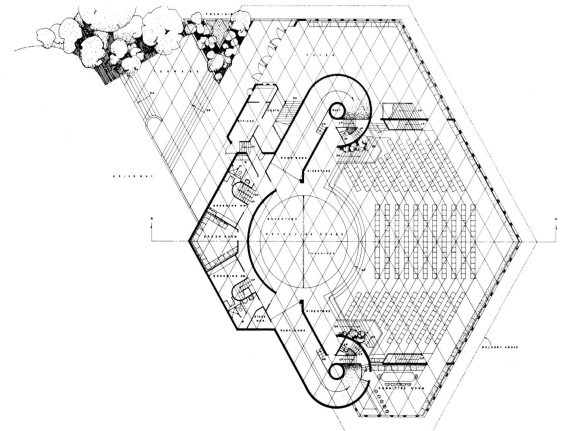

77 Groundplan.

78 Auditorium and
   light bridge
   as seen from the
   stage.

79 The auditorium,
   facing the stage.

80 Exterior view of model.

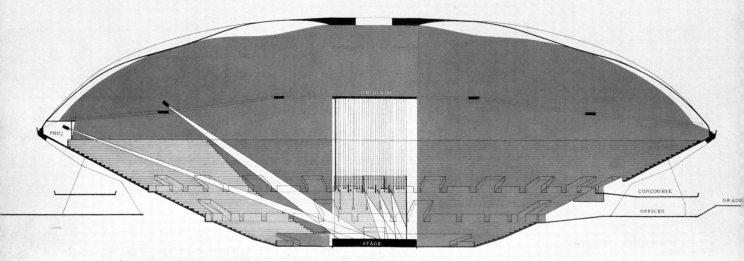

81 Section view of the theatre.

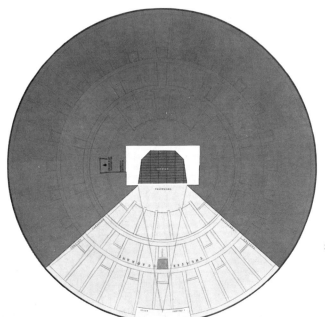

82 Theatrical plan.

University of Illinois Assembly Hall,
Urbana, Illinois.
Harrison and Abramovitz,
architects.

Two new American arts
centers built around an
opera house.

83 Project for a National
   Cultural Center on the
   Potomac River
   in Washington, D.C.

84 The Lincoln Center for
   the Performing Arts in
   New York;
   Wallace K. Harrison,
   chief architect.

85 Mozart's *Così fan tutte* at the Metropolitan Opera. Production staged by Alfred Lunt and designed by Rolf Gérard.

86 Robert Edmond Jones' design for the American première of Alban Berg's *Wozzeck* in Philadelphia, 1931. ▶

87 Scene from *Susannah*, by Carlisle Floyd; New York City Opera Company production with Andreas Nomikos as designer.

86

87

88
Andrea Chenier,
Act I, at the
Cincinnati
Summer
Opera;
designed by
Wolfgang
Roth.

89
*The Wise
Maiden*,
by Carl Orff,
at the Karamu
Theatre
in Cleveland.
The pro-
duction was
done by Benno
D. Frank.

90 The auditorium.

Opera at Indiana University (Bloomington, Indiana).

91 First scenic production in America of Handel's oratorio *Belshazzar* (1959). Scenery by C. M. Cristini.

92 Puccini's *Sister Angelica* as presented by the Curtis Institute of Music and the University of Pennsylvania in Philadelphia.

93 Scene from a production of Purcell's *Dido and Aeneas* at the University of Washington in Seattle. Here the witches and sailors are performing in front of a projected background.

94 Opera on television: The Metropolitan Opera production, by Garson Kanin, of *Die Fledermaus*, re-staged for the Ford Foundation's *Omnibus* program, CBS-Television, New York, 1953.

95 More opera on television:
Marriage of Figaro, Act III,
as produced by the NBC
Opera Company,
New York.

96 Opera on film:
A scene from Verdi's
La Traviata, produced by
Gregor Rabinovitch
under the title
"The Lost One"
(Columbia Pictures)

3. ARTISTIC POLICY

The professional opera company in America, whether of the "Grand" or the community type, lacks not only an opera house but also financial security. This makes it impossible to pursue an artistic policy which would guarantee its personnel an assured artistic and economic existence. The unstable foundations of sponsorship do not permit the management of most companies to plan beyond one season; and the season itself is usually far too short to build up companies comparable to those in Europe.

Short seasons

The major companies, except for the Metropolitan, operate for a maximum of only ten or twelve weeks. Operas are repeated two or three times. Operatic solo artists are not able to make a living as members of one operatic organization, except for those employed by the Metropolitan; and not even all Metropolitan artists can survive on Metropolitan contracts alone. No opera company, with the exception of the Metropolitan, is in a position to write contracts providing an annual living wage to members of the orchestra, chorus, ballet and technical staff.

It is not surprising, under these circumstances, that unions and managers try to exact conditions that make the operation of an operatic organization extremely difficult. At the same time, solo artists and chorus have the hard task of performing in four different languages, and usually under the strain of insufficient preparation due to limited rehearsal time.

"Bread-and-butter" operas

The repertory is for the most part limited to well-known bread-and-butter operas, with the financial risk of rare, old or modern works undertaken only occasionally. During the period between 1950 and 1959 the Metropolitan Opera performed only two works written in recent years—Strawinsky's *Rake's Progress* and the Barber-Menotti *Vanessa*. Recent grants by the Ford Foundation have made it possible for the four major opera companies to produce modern American operas, but contemporary foreign opera is still left to the initiative of opera workshops or to occasional individual efforts.

Opera in English?

Except for some instances, mainly in the field of comic opera, standard operas are not generally performed in English by professional American opera companies. This reminds me of an incident that happened years ago at the Metropolitan. Bruno Walter was conducting *Fidelio* in English, and I was the stage director. After scoring a rather debatable success, Bruno Walter remarked a little plaintively, "The foreigners seem to be the only ones who *really* want opera to be given in English, don't you think?"

Star system
Because the star system is followed by the major professional companies, and foreign artists are in great demand, it is difficult at times to give opera in English. New American singers are to an increasing extent, however, taking their place on an equal footing with foreign artists, and today many Europeans are able to sing in English. Another problem is the unhappy shortage of adequate English translations of foreign operas. The problem of translation exists also in Europe, of course, but there it has never been considered a serious obstacle to the general practice of performing opera in the language of the audience.

One consequence of the prevailing star system is the complete lack of a permanent operatic ensemble. Even in new productions at the Metropolitan, the turnover of the cast and, more recently, of stage directors as well, is so rapid that before long only scenery and costumes remain as a memento of the original production. Often new singers replace the original leads without stage rehearsal. In the third performance of my new production of *Don Giovanni* at the Metropolitan, for instance, there were four new leading artists in the cast, while my contract as stage director terminated with the première. In five performances of my staging of *Rigoletto* I counted four different Gildas, four Dukes and three Rigolettos.

Once a well-known artist arrived for a rehearsal on the roof stage of the Metropolitan, where there is no scenery, to prepare his Metropolitan debut in a familiar role. He refused to accept my direction under the circumstances. He explained that he would be glad to change his conception of the part if he had adequate stage rehearsal, but he was afraid that with one rehearsal on this makeshift stage he would not be able to do justice either to himself or to me. It would only result in a performance unsatisfactory to us both. I could not but find his viewpoint fully justified and gave him freedom to perform the role in his own way. This seemed the only course to take, particularly since it involved the debut of a very artistic personality.

European opera houses, as we saw above, employ either the repertory or the *stagione* system. Under the repertory system, used in German-speaking countries, a great number of operas are, in theory, permanently available for performance. Under the *stagione* system, used in Italy, one opera is given several performances

130

within a short period and is then followed by another work, which is also repeated a number of times. The repertory system, properly speaking, requires a permanent personnel for the entire season. In contrast, under the *stagione* system, solo artists and directors are employed for shorter periods covering the rehearsals and performances of only one work.

The repertory system and its handicaps

The Metropolitan follows the repertory system in scheduling performances, but it does not have the necessary control over its ensemble to make the system work. Because of the short-term contracts of leading artists, casts are changing constantly. This same practice is destroying the traditional repertory system of the major German-speaking opera companies. But the Met has an additional problem—its short season. The year-round season of German-speaking opera houses is interrupted only by a six-week vacation. The Metropolitan has a lay-off of more than six months after the end of the New York season. The Metropolitan tour, with performances on stages of various sizes, necessary changes in the production, and no time for rehearsals, obviously does not help hold the productions together. As a result, in every new season even works well established in the repertory must, for all practical purposes, be restaged.

On the other hand, the *stagione* system would not solve the Metropolitan's problem either, for it would conflict with the present subscription system, which requires that the same opera be performed from time to time throughout the season. Most other American opera companies, which present only two or three performances of a work (if not merely one!), in effect are employing the *stagione* system. Unfortunately, however, the all-too-few repeat performances do not make possible a satisfactory amortization of the effort and expense involved.

Limited number of new productions

High production costs and small returns force the American opera manager to be careful with his outlay for new productions. The Metropolitan puts on an average of four new productions a year. La Scala stages fifteen to twenty during a season of comparable length, and a smaller opera house like the Zurich Stadttheater puts on fifteen new productions during a season of ten and one-half months. Very few opera companies in America have their own facilities for making scenery, costumes, properties and wigs. This does not improve the economics of American operatic production. During recent years new productions at the Metropolitan and the Chicago Lyric Opera have been made possible only by gifts from individuals, opera guilds and foundations. More recently the import and exchange of scenery was initiated by Chicago and Dallas to alleviate the situation, and at the present time the major American opera companies are discussing the possibilities of the exchange of productions among themselves.

The major opera companies in the United States can manage only a limited number of new productions, but with the smaller groups the situation is still worse. They have to rely to a great extent on rented scenery and costumes. They are lucky if they have an artistic house nearby, such as Peter Wolf Associates at Dallas, which furnishes productions to companies in Texas and nearby states. Others make their own productions with simple means, and yet often with reasonably satisfactory results. Still others, and I am afraid this includes the majority of professional groups, are satisfied with, or have to be satisfied with, scenery and costumes which can hardly win new friends for opera among our movie-trained audiences.

The anxiety to avoid any risk and the desire to appeal to the average theatre-goer influences not only choice of repertory, but also style of operatic production. As in the commercial Broadway theatre, scenery and costumes of a traditional, realistic type are preferred to a modern "experiment." Well-established "name" designers as well as fledgling artists bow to this unwritten rule. Outstanding modern painters and architects rarely find a chance to participate, and if they do take part they are seriously restricted by union regulations.

Conservative production style Notable theatre and film directors and designers have been brought to the Metropolitan by Rudolf Bing, it is true, and production standards have been raised. Opera singers are losing weight and learning to act. Nevertheless, even in the relatively few new productions at the Metropolitan a rather old-fashioned approach prevails. Characteristically, designs for new Metropolitan productions by such notable European figures as Caspar Neher reflect productions done in Europe years ago. Teo Otto's *Tristan* at the Metropolitan, strangely enough, was considered "provocative" by the American press. Other new productions conceived in a clearly realistic manner were received with unqualified enthusiasm. In contrast, the simple, imaginative stage designs of R. E. Jones, Bel Geddes, Oenslager and Simonson, though created many years ago, seem very "modern" in comparison with what is being done now. The present determination is to "play it safe." This policy is dictated by economic rather than artistic considerations.

Out-dated stages Other deterents to better operatic productions are the lack of a modern stage, the shortage of storage space, the necessity for tours and the problems of scheduling. At the Metropolitan, for instance, the Saturday matinee performance of an opera may end at six o'clock in the afternoon, with another opera scheduled to appear on the same stage two hours later. It is obvious that when a new production is conceived, all these circumstances must be taken into account.

Lighting presents similar complications. One often hears criticism of the lighting at the Metropolitan. But consider the problems faced by the lighting technicians. Within a period of six days, these men must handle five stage rehearsals and six performances of different operas in New York, plus, perhaps, one performance of an additional work in Philadelphia. Can they be expected to achieve perfect lighting throughout each of these performances, or utilize a complicated system of modern spotlights? It seems obvious that a make-do system of production and lighting has to be adopted which can hardly be expected to bear comparison with the run-of-the-play set-up of a Broadway production.

Lack of rehearsals Most of these production problems do not exist in European opera theatres. The most vital difference lies in the availability of stage rehearsal time in Europe, and rehearsals are essential to make an operatic performance live. Much as this situation has improved recently at the Metropolitan, especially in the case of new productions, the rehearsal schedule cannot be compared with that available under European conditions, nor with that employed in preparing a Broadway production. Nor is the situation improved by the problems already mentioned— changes of cast, touring, and lay-off during the summer months. Rehearsal schedules for operas which are not new productions are unbelievably modest.

For my opening production of *Otello* in Zurich there were eighteen stage rehearsals with piano, and eight with orchestra. At the Metropolitan, for a new production the maximum number of stage rehearsals with piano was seven. In Italy a production is taken out of the repertory after one or two seasons. In German-speaking countries it may be kept for about five years. An American production must last considerably longer. The American operatic stage director in charge of restaging an average production will usually be allowed, at best, one or two stage rehearsals with piano. Often there is *no* stage rehearsal. The director's accomplishments under these circumstances are frequently just short of miraculous. No less astonishing are the performances of the young American operatic artists who, despite these handicaps, often turn out excellent performances.

Artistic direction takes second place

Since financial considerations are of such decisive importance in the conduct and survival of an American opera company, the manager is usually chosen primarily with an eye to his administrative talents, rather than his artistic qualifications. In America, as in England, conductors and stage directors have little, if any, influence on the formation of artistic policy. Many important permanent conductors of the Metropolitan have left the company for this reason. Guest directors may have some authority over their own productions, but they cannot very well interfere with repertory productions. The executive manager rather than the artist is in control.

The situation is different in Europe. In Italy artistic policy is controlled by an artistic director, working with the *sovrintendente*. The Italian artistic director is usually a composer; in Vienna he is a conductor; and in Germany, a stage director. What would Vienna have been without Gustav Mahler and Richard Strauss? How would La Scala have fared without Toscanini? Or, in the present time, try to imagine Bayreuth without Wieland and Wolfgang Wagner.

Disregard for the artist in the formulation of artistic policy is certainly one of the most damaging consequences of the precarious position in which American professional opera companies find themselves. This situation, of course, is the direct result of imitating a European system of operatic production without benefit of the corresponding European system of sponsorship.

New American artistic policy needed

But the growing interest of the American public in opera, the enthusiasm of American sponsors and producers of opera, the wealth and ability of American operatic talent, as well as the emergence of American civic opera companies and art centers, will in the end inevitably lead to the only possible solution: the establishment of an artistic policy based on the unique conditions which opera faces in the United States.

4. OPERA SCHOOLS

The clouds which hover over the professional opera companies in America lift as soon as we turn to the field of opera schools. In the secure atmosphere of the academic world we find a new form of operatic life developing; opera has become a recognized and subsidized educational activity. This development goes far beyond its counterpart in Europe and holds infinite promise for the future of opera in the United States.

The three types of operatic training

Three major types of operatic activity in the field of education are:

1. *Opera departments of conservatories.* In the opera schools of the Peabody Conservatory at Baltimore, the Eastman School of Music in Rochester, the Cincinnati Conservatory of Music, the Curtis Institute of Music in Philadelphia, the Juilliard School of Music, and about twenty-five other conservatories, operatic training is available the year around on a professional level, based on curriculums similar to those in European music schools.

2. *Opera workshops*, sponsored chiefly by, or in connection with universities and colleges. The workshop is a new type of opera school which developed as a uniquely American project, originating about the time World War II began. This movement is still growing. The number of opera workshops on an educational level throughout the United States is now about 200.

3. *Educational opera companies*, the logical off-spring of opera workshops and closely connected with them. These companies were formed in order to provide workshops and schools with a wider audience and are important germ cells for the formation of professional civic opera companies.

Different aims

The first type of activity, the opera department of the conservatory, does not face any particular problems since its entire program is devoted exclusively to professional training of the student. The second type, the university and college workshop, however, is confronted with a grave dilemma: Should primary emphasis be placed upon strictly professional training, or upon the more academic aspects of the university or college curriculum? Some schools concentrate on professional training. The opera department of Indiana University in Bloomington, for example, is for all practical purposes a self-contained professional opera center. Other schools look upon their opera departments as academic ventures designed to broaden interest in this branch of the liberal arts. That is the aim of operatic study at the University of Kansas at Lawrence, Kansas, for instance, as stated by its former Chancellor, Franklin D. Murphy.

On a visit to this school in 1958, soon after the opening of its new Music and Dramatic Arts Building, I witnessed a fine performance of Menotti's *The Saint of Bleecker Street*. Mr. Murphy explained at that time, "While we aim to train some singers, instrumentalists, and particularly teachers for professional careers, our major purpose is to train our new academic citizen, the doctor, the scientist, to go back to his daily work with an experience of and desire for the better things in life. In this way he will become a moving force within his community in influencing his fellow citizen and finally his congressmen to solicit public assistance for artistic purposes. And in this manner we will, by truly democratic process, gradually build up interest and active support for the arts."

Between these two extremes—concentration on training for an operatic career on a professional level and concern with opera as a purely academic function—there is a wide range of possibilities for the operation of a university or college opera workshop. Experienced leaders in this field usually try to reach a reasonable compromise.

Peter Paul Fuchs, for instance, conductor of opera and symphony at the Louisiana State University at Baton Rouge, Louisiana, summarized the existing positive facts and needs as follows: "I do not believe that too many reforms are necessary in the field of college opera. College opera at its best can, I think, be very good, particularly when you consider the fact that it must work encumbered by the natural limitations of school surroundings and requirements. For example, no teacher of opera can conscientiously ask that his students drop all other activities in order to be available for all the rehearsals that he deems necessary. I think that with all its compromises this field has produced very remarkable results.

"On the other hand, I do believe that all our available energies should be devoted to the creation of professional opera groups worthy of receiving the best talent that is being trained in our colleges. Our students must have a place to go after we finish training them, and our audiences must be given a type of professional opera that needs no apologies but nevertheless makes direct contact with them—in short, does not try to emulate the Metropolitan Opera."

The opera workshop, despite its shortcomings, is the most important factor in America when it comes to providing young operatic artists with an opportunity to gain practical training through performance and experimentation. The workshop in this sense has become, to a certain extent, the American substitute for the Middle-European small opera theatre.

I have put on workshop performances myself, and attended others. However, in order to gain a comprehensive picture of how American opera schools and workshops operate, I sent out questionnaires, with the assistance of the Central Opera Service, to 200 groups throughout the United States and Canada. One hundred and twenty-five of these groups supplied generous information. On the basis of their replies I will try to summarize workshop methods.

Professional or academic interest?

The conservatories of music state that all their operatic students plan to become professionals and are not primarily interested in academic work. The university and college workshops show a preponderance of participants who intend to make opera their career, although most of these young people are at the same time interested in academic work as well. In reply to the question, "Does your group include students who plan to become operatic professionals?" 61 per cent of the workshop groups responded with an unqualified "Yes," 27 per cent with a partial "Yes" (and a few probably more realistic teachers added, "Some hope to"), and only 12 per cent with an outspoken "No." The question, "Do you use students who have primarily academic interest?" was answered by 64 per cent with "Yes," 27 per cent with a partial "Yes," and 9 per cent with a definite "No."

If we add to this workshop breakdown the opera students from the regular musical conservatories, we arrive at the astonishing conclusion that almost two-thirds of the students performing opera in the academic field hope to make opera their professional career. It is hard to confront these ambitious and often very talented thousands of young students with the practical realities existing today in the operatic field, either in the United States or abroad.

Repertory

Supported by educational funds and unhampered by union restrictions, opera workshops are free of the basic limitations which hamper struggling professional opera companies. This is reflected in the choice of repertory as well as in the number of rehearsals provided. Opera workshops in general do not restrict themselves to sure-fire repertory works, but also present rarely-produced old works as well as modern works, ranging from Monteverdi to Menotti and Bernstein. The informative annual survey, "U.S. Opera Compass," published by the Metropolitan Opera Guild's *Opera News*, points out that contemporary operas make up more than half the list of operatic productions given annually in the United States and receive well over half the total performances. The survey covering 1958–59 reports: "Last season the U.S. heard 2,084 performances of 165 modern operas, overwhelmingly by American composers, and only 1,871 performances of 116 traditional works."* These figures obviously reflect the activity of opera workshops.

While the directors of many opera workshops give primary emphasis to contemporary opera, others base their work almost entirely on the proven masterpieces. Josef Blatt, Director of Opera Production at the University of Michigan in Ann Arbor declares, "As this is part of a school, our productions aim to give the student a thorough training in the fields of operatic singing and acting. The emphasis lies on understanding of principles and on learning ways to study and apply oneself to this art beyond the requirements of the particular role. I feel that only masterworks can give a student the challenge needed for the growth of his or her talent. The principles of our production are to achieve utmost aliveness and intensity, dramatically, and at the same time, unfailing precision and faithfulness to the score. Experience has shown that the artistic development of the student induces a parallel growth of his vocal abilities."

Arthur G. Cosenza of the Opera Workshop at Loyola University in New Orleans seconds him by stating, "Since it is my belief that college students who intend to become opera singers should have knowledge of the standard repertoire, the greatest part of our work consists of scenes from the standard operas."

Indiana University

The operation of the workshops ranges from an ambitious operatic schedule, which may include several operas performed with orchestra, to the presentation of a single opera with piano. Bloomington produces from seven to nine complete operas yearly with orchestra, in two theatres seating 3,750 and 1,100. The program includes an annual production of *Parsifal* at Easter. The Bloomington School has on its faculty a number of prominent conductors, stage directors and voice teachers; and in addition it has its own scenic department, with well-known guest designers such as Crayon, Nomikos, and C. M. Cristini from the San Carlo Opera in Naples.

* *Opera News*, November 14, 1959.

I know from my own experience the excellent operatic work being done by the School of Music at Indiana University. In November, 1959, I staged the first American scenic performance of Handel's oratorio *Belshazzar* with the forces of this school. Tibor Kozma, formerly of the Metropolitan Opera, conducted, and C. M. Cristini was the designer. About 200 students took part in the performance. For this production two up-to-date projection machines were imported from Germany. In every respect this presentation would hold its own with any given by a European Stadttheater.

Opera at U.S.C.

The University of Southern California has the same high professional operatic aims. Walter Ducloux, Director of the Department of Opera (which Carl Ebert earlier brought to recognition), summarized these high goals as follows:

"American leadership in opera! Stage-directors who can read and interpret a score. Conductors who can visualize a dramatic sequence on stage. Composers willing to put the spotlight where it must be in the theatre—on the singer-actor—and who realize that absolute pitch can never replace expressive and powerful singing as a communicative factor. Increasing effort to promote opera in English. Better training in enunciation in English. A constant fight to abolish the double standard of values in appraising performances—professional equals good, amateur equals bad. A growing awareness that a young American singer of twenty-five need not be less talented or more childish than his European counterpart.

"Future plans—a five-year Verdi cycle. We are steering unceasingly toward large-scale works in order to develop a potential in orchestra, chorus, and ballet. Within five years our orchestra and regular opera chorus ought to number over 100. They, more than the soloists, are the standard-bearers of opera."

By this time the Opera Department under Ducloux, who acts as his own translator, conductor and stage director, is well on its way, with Verdi's *Don Carlo*, *Falstaff*, *Otello* and *Simone Boccanegra* already produced.

At UCLA

While the Opera Workshop of U.S.C. gives one full production of proven masterworks each semester—and the possibility of obtaining a degree in opera, as is the case at Indiana University—its competitive counterpart at UCLA (University of California at Los Angeles) carries on an extensive program devoted frequently to contemporary and rarely-heard operas.

The UCLA Opera Workshop was founded by Jan Popper, who recently organ-

139

ized a similar workshop on the Berkeley campus of the University. During the 1958–59 school year, with Wolfgang Martin as Musical Director and Lotfollah Mansouri as Stage Director, the Workshop produced six operas, three in each semester. There were a total of twenty-one regular performances, plus a series of "Opera Highlight" performances.

Mansouri explains, "Our policy has been to present new operas or rarely-performed classical works in full-length productions. The 'Highlight' programs are the culmination of the semester's work and include scenes from standard repertoire operas. In this way the Workshop accomplishes a two-fold purpose: It provides the facilities for learning and performing roles in the standard works, and it presents to the public operas of unusual interest, which they might not ordinarily get a chance to see."

Other opera workshops In addition to the workshops of U.S.C. and UCLA, there is their predecessor, the Los Angeles City College Opera Workshop under Hugo Strelitzer.

Looking to the north, we find Stanley Chapple, who at the Opera Workshop of the University of Washington produced fifteen performances of eight operas during the 1958–59 academic year. Brigham Young University at Provo, Utah, normally produces four or five operas a year. Josef Blatt at the Opera Workshop of the University of Michigan; designer-director Elemer Nagy at Hart College, Hartford, Connecticut; and the University of Louisiana State—all put on three operas a year. The Juilliard School of Music, where Frederic Cohen stages interesting productions, and the Eastman School of Music Opera Theatre, at Rochester, New York, under Leonard Treash, present usually one to four operas a year. The Peabody Conservatory in Baltimore, with its Art Theatre under Laszlo Halasz, produces several operas each year. Most opera workshops, however, perform no more than one or two operas yearly.

In general, opera workshops put on productions in English when they perform entire operas. Individual scenes from operas are presented both in English and in the original languages.

Collaboration between departments Many universities have encouraged an active collaboration between music department, opera workshop and other departments such as speech, drama and physical education. All too rarely is there active co-operation between the opera workshop and the young talent of the fine arts department. I had a most happy surprise, however, at the University of Pennsylvania. Here student painters from the Fine Arts Department of the University joined forces with the Curtis Institute of Music to put on an evening of two operas. Rarely have I seen more promising projects for scenery and costumes than those presented by the twelve competing young artists, who were unhampered by operatic "tradition." My only problem was to choose two from among so many excellent proposals, for realization in actual performance.

Style of production

Workshop productions usually aim at simplicity in scenery and costumes. This not only helps economically, but also serves artistic purposes. So wrote Mr. B. L. Gibson, Conductor of the Opera Workshop of Berea College in Berea, Kentucky: "We have had some very successful college productions with mere suggestions of a set and use costumes from the Dramatics Department. Expenses have been kept to a minimum this way. We find that the result is *toward* effectiveness rather than away from it."

Ludwig Zirner from the University of Illinois Opera Group adds: "We use our own convertible costumes and scenic elements for programs of scenes as well as for complete productions. By adding to our existing stock from year to year we are now in a position to mount almost any work with considerable economy. We find that in most cases a simplified conception of scenery, properties and costumes stimulates the imagination of the performers and the audience; this approach is not only more economical but keeps productions light and flexible." What Mr. Zirner does not mention is the fact that his wife, Laura Zirner, published an original book on costume designs based on unit patterns.*

While opera workshops usually make their own scenery, often working together with the drama departments, they frequently rent costumes from costume companies. There appears to be little inclination to undertake scenic experimentation in workshop opera production. Nearly all presentations are put on within the traditional proscenium frame. Only in a few instances are there attempts to play opera in the arena style, as is done occasionally at Baton Rouge, Louisiana, and the University of New Mexico in Albuquerque. Other groups which have experimented with this type of production are the workshops of Northwest Missouri State College, the State College of Stevens Point, Wisconsin, and Drake University at Des Moines, Iowa. The Opera Workshop of Chatham,

* Laura Zirner, *Costuming for the Modern Stage* (Urbana: University of Illinois Press, 1957).

in Pittsburgh, Pennsylvania, looks forward to working in the revolutionary new Carnegie Theatre. Workshop opera in general, however, remains, like professional opera, more conservative than its relative, the dramatic theatre.

There has been some experimentation with new materials and techniques, such as Fiberglas and aluminum scenery (Boris Goldovsky and Elemer Nagy), corrugated cardboard scenery (Duquesne University at Pittsburgh) and projected scenery (University of Washington in Seattle). Concerning these efforts, Frederic Cohen of Juilliard observes: "What is most needed in this field is artistic imagination and an honest professional approach to all artistic problems of opera. This basic attitude seems to me a much more important need than all the technical gimmicks such as Fiberglas, projection of scenery, TV performances, and the like."

Television and film

And yet television plays an increasingly important part in the thinking and planning of opera workshops. Twenty-five per cent of the workshops appear on educational television and, at times, also local commercial stations, or at least they occasionally transmit operatic scenes. During the summer of 1959, the Music Academy of the West, in Santa Barbara, California, instituted an opera workshop for TV under my direction, with the active co-operation of the local television station. On Saturdays I staged opera scenes in a public master class before an invited audience at the Academy, and the following day repeated the same scenes over TV from the television studio, making the changes required by the medium. This proved an interesting experience for both the students and the audience.

Opera on film is not so often attempted yet as part of normal workshop activity, although there are already instances of it. Films have been made by the University of Alabama "Opera à la Bama" Workshop, and by Goldovsky at Pittsburgh's Station WTED, among others.

Budget and rehearsals

Most workshops operate without fees and without using union members. A few groups pay the technical crew and any additional local musicians who are needed to supplement the student orchestra. The cost of workshop productions is usually covered by income from the sale of low-priced tickets, with the sponsoring educational institution paying the deficit. Since they are not subject to union fees and regulations, opera workshops can prepare their productions slowly and carefully.

142

Eastman's Opera Theatre reports 150 hours of stage rehearsals with piano for "an average production," and approximately nine with orchestra. Missouri State College lists "100 hours over three months, mostly with piano, ten with orchestra." Baylor University at Waco, Texas, has thirty to fifty stage rehearsals with piano, and twelve to fifteen with orchestra, in order to prepare one opera. The University of Southern California allows twenty to thirty with piano, eight to ten with orchestra. Juilliard has twenty stage rehearsals with piano, eight to twelve with orchestra; and the Curtis Institute of Music has twenty on stage with piano and fourteen with orchestra. Other non-professional operatic groups follow more or less the same pattern.

What is needed? What is most-needed in this field? Replies to this question can be summarized as follows:

1. Good translations of standard operas.
2. Readily available musical material, particularly in the field of smaller operas.
3. "A book concerning appropriate excerpts for workshop productions."
4. Good, workable, lively "prompt books" of other productions for study.
5. Technical improvement of theatres:
   a) First, a sufficiently large orchestra pit.
   b) Modern lighting facilities.
   c) Larger stages, more space backstage and for storage, "fly" space, cycloramas and acoustical improvements.

Some workshop leaders summarize their most important needs as "money" or "funds;" others, as "everything."

Jan Popper, of the University of California, makes the following observations:

"1. We have found stylized or suggested sets and costumes very useful for the presentation of opera excerpts.
2. On evenings of opera excerpts we have found informal narration between scenes very helpful to:
   a) Cover the scene change,
   b) Inform and educate the audience (without their feeling that they are being 'educated').
3. We have found that we can do much effective staging with lights and curtains, without cumbersome sets, even in full productions.

4. Our stage director and stage designer, as well as the rest of the production staff, are employed by the Music Department, which enables us to do our planning without interference or inter-departmental 'red tape.'

5. Students can be regularly enrolled or can enter through the University Extension Division as 'special' students. We find that mixing undergraduates with more experienced 'special' students is very commendable.

6. We find that one full production annually of a new American work is very stimulating to both students and audiences. (Not to speak about the stimulus to U.S. opera production!)."

While there are many different opinions about the best method of operating an opera workshop, none will disagree with Ludwig Zirner's definition of the needs in this field: "Better and more civic opera organizations. More collaboration between orchestras and opera groups. Better musicians, more imaginative stage directors. More and better theatres."

Oberlin's Opera Laboratory observes, "Greatest need—some place besides the Met for our graduates to grow and get experience while earning a living! The Met tour has killed off local enterprise in many cities. More regional activity is needed. Perhaps government subsidy is the answer."

Vernon Hammond, Director of the Academy of Vocal Arts in Philadelphia, compresses definition of the chief need into the formula: "Decentralized professional opera companies." Since this remains indeed the most important goal, we follow with particular interest the process by which civic opera companies branch off from opera schools and collaborate with them until finally they stand on their own feet.

From opera workshop to civic opera company

This was the case with Boris Goldovsky's New England Opera Theatre, which originated at the New England Conservatory. Across the border we see the impressive growth of the Canadian Opera Company under the direction of Herman Geiger-Tourel. Beginning with a group in the Opera School of the Conservatory in Toronto in 1946, a Royal Conservatory Opera Company developed which was still being sponsored by the School as late as 1950. In 1951, the administration was taken over by a citizens' committee; and in 1954 the company became The Opera Festival Company of Toronto. By now it is the fully professional Canadian Opera Company, enjoying financial support from private donations as well as from the Canada Council. It received $60,000

144

from the Council in 1958 and presents opera throughout Canada as well as in Toronto.

The development from school groups to civic opera groups usually starts within the school itself. For instance, at Bob Jones University in Greenville, South Carolina, the Bob Jones University Opera Association was founded in 1942. The organization of this group has been described by Dwight Gustafson, Dean of the School of Fine Arts, as follows:

"We are a self-sustaining organization and draw our talent for orchestra, chorus and directing positions from our own student body and faculty. The Music Department and the Department of Dramatic Production co-operate for our opera performances, and our stage director is usually a member of our speech faculty. I have been conducting the performances with assistance of chorus masters from the University faculty. Our sets and costumes are designed and executed by members of the University staff with the assistance of students who do the work as part of a work-loan scholarship arrangement. Because we offer instruction in music, speech, and art without additional cost above our academic tuition, many students participate in these productions who are not majoring in the fields of music and speech but who are receiving training in those fields. A number of the students are music majors; however, we do not have a program for the training of operatic professionals.

"We present at least one complete opera each season with two performances. Quite often we schedule two operas. One of these usually is in English, utilizing our own students and faculty in the leading roles. In at least one production a year, we feature guest artists in the leading roles. We also feature operatic scenes in our Commencement Concert. This year we have presented Verdi's *Il Trovatore* and will present Act IV of Puccini's *La Bohème*. We usually have twelve to fifteen stage rehearsals with piano and six stage rehearsals with orchestra for a major production. Our theatre is a proscenium type and has a seating capacity of approximately 2,800.

"We have not televised our performances. However, several short scenes have been filmed by our cinema production unit, 'Unusual Films', which produces educational and religious films."

The next step for the educational opera organization is to extend its hand to other civic groups in active collaboration. This development we can see taking place as described in a report from the Texas Western College Opera Company at El Paso. Its conductor, Dr. E. A. Thormodsgaard, writes:

"Our new plan, coordinating college and civic efforts, is to keep down expenses by using the college facilities—rehearsal rooms, costumes, scenery, auditorium and the college orchestra. A large percentage of any profits (above a $1000 sustaining fund and expenses) goes to the City Symphony in the form of Orchestra Scholarships to be given to college students. This encourages City Symphony interest too. All city voice teachers are included on a rotating membership basis in the auditioning committee, each serving through one production at a time."

In a similar way the Opera Guild at Tallahassee, Florida, gains from co-operation with the Florida State University since all its directors and the business manager are paid by the University. Only the accompanist and the expenses of the physical production are paid out of gate receipts, and this cost averages about $1,800 for two performances of one opera.

The Beaumont Opera Workshop in Beaumont, Texas, under the direction of its founder, Joseph Truncale, stages productions jointly with the Lamar State College of Technology. It considers itself a community group: "Actually, we are a civic organization producing opera on a shoestring, for the sheer love of it. We are fortunate enough to have talented and enthusiastic amateurs for our chorus, gifted professionals who are willing to donate their time to sing solo roles, and an artistic director who can and does do everything from singing the tenor lead to sweeping the stage after the sets are struck!

"All of the directors and many of the singers are affiliated with Lamar Tech, which has been most generous in providing facilities free of charge. Under our current agreement with the College they provide auditorium and rehearsal space, and the workshop has been set up as a special course to be included in Mr. Truncale's teaching schedule. Dr. Skinner, Mr. Wiley, and other faculty members donate their time to conduct, direct staging, etc.

"Necessary finances are raised by the Beaumont Opera Workshop, with the provision that all money above a set operating budget be put into a scholarship fund to be administered by the College. In addition, the Beaumont Opera Workshop has for two years awarded a partial scholarship to one of its own members."

146

Thus, in many places throughout America, opera companies are gradually developing from elementary workshops in the field of education into semi-professional or professional organizations which are happy to co-operate with interested groups in their own or neighboring communities. This process of development may seem primitive and difficult, but it is nevertheless a practical, organized means of growth towards the desired end—professional civic opera companies.

And what comes after the training?

Let us not mistake the means for the end itself, however. America's investment in opera schools and workshops is not yet paying the dividends it should. Quite the contrary. Most of its young operatic artists do not know where to turn for employment when they have finished their training. "The majority of the students," concludes Mansouri, former Stage Director at UCLA, "upon leaving, have to go to Europe. There are no opportunities for a full-time career in California, unless they are satisfied with singing in studio choruses or in the choruses of the many television shows emanating from Hollywood. The few opera performances by local groups are on too meager a scale to support so many talented young singers in the city."

The same thing is true for the rest of the country. Private, governmental and foundation scholarships offer some valuable assistance to the exodus of American operatic talent. The Fulbright Student Program and the Baird-Rockefeller Aid to Music Program, for instance, help many young operatic artists get to Europe, but only a few of them find employment. And yet, even those who are established look back to America hoping that eventually there will be opera companies at home able to take care of their artistic and financial needs.

Need for collaboration between opera school and professional opera company

Opera schools and workshops are important means to this end. In due course America must establish a comprehensive working relationship between year-round opera workshops and professional opera companies, with the opera companies drawing upon workshop talents. As we have seen, this kind of practical production-line for operatic personnel once existed at Naples, Paris, Milan and Florence, and was proposed in Wagner's project of the ideal opera organization. But for the present let us be grateful that opera schools and workshops do exist in such numbers and of such quality. They are becoming increasingly significant elements in the creation of an American civic opera.

5. OPERA ON TELEVISION

First opera telecasts in America
In the United States, opera and television became friends as soon as the new medium started. On March 10, 1940, the first operatic telecast was transmitted from the studios of the National Broadcasting Company in Radio City, New York. On that historic occasion, Frank St. Leger conducted a group of Metropolitan artists in the first act of *Pagliacci*, and Edward Johnson acted as Master of Ceremonies. Three years later General Electric's television station at Schenectady, New York, began the production of operas.

In 1944, I was appointed Director of Operatic Production for NBC in New York, at a time when there were only a few thousand television sets in private use. From the small Studio 3-H we transmitted various operatic scenes and condensed versions of operas on an experimental basis. Even in those early days the audience showed great interest in opera, rating it third after sports and news.

The following years witnessed a fabulous growth of television in the United States; the number of receiving sets increased within ten years from a few thousand to more than fifty million. Today, apparently, there are more American homes with TV receivers than with bathtubs.* NBC in New York soon set up its own TV Opera Company with Samuel Chotzinoff as producer, Peter Herman Adler as artistic and musical director and Kirk Browning as TV director. Browning has been responsible for staging most of the excellent operatic studio telecasts which have been presented regularly for more than a decade. Productions have included not only standard operas, but also contemporary works. Except for the annual production of Menotti's *Amahl and the Night Visitors*, which was commissioned by NBC-TV, and a few other productions, however, the NBC Opera Company did not find commercial sponsorship. It has been carried on a sustaining basis.

Conflicts with commercial sponsorship
In contrast to NBC's generous sponsorship, the other television networks produce opera only on rare occasions. Thus opera on television in the United States, except for the NBC Opera Company, has been restricted to popular operatic excerpts which are commercially acceptable as ingredients in potpourri

* According to *Teaching by Television*, a joint publication of the Ford Foundation and the Fund for the Advancement of Education (New York, May, 1959).

programs of musical "entertainment." These programs have ranged from NBC's "Producer's Showcase" spectaculars to Ed Sullivan's not-always-happy experiments with opera.

Professional opera directors who become involved in such programs usually have to subject themselves to unending compromises which approach the trials that directors of operatic sequences for Hollywood films have to face. For example, when putting on a nationwide telecast of the first act of *La Bohème*, I had to bow to the omission of the voices of Rodolfo's friends during the duet of Mimi and Rodolfo; the twenty seconds in which the two expensive stars, Tebaldi and Björling, did not sing, seemed a waste of money to the producer. Another producer wanted me to insert a Viennese Valse into *La Traviata* to make life in the third act a bit gayer. Such experiences ended for me this otherwise very pleasant and lucrative activity.

Assets of operatic TV production The NBC Opera Company productions developed a television technique that clearly demonstrates the great possibilities that this medium offers. Opera on television can be believable as dramatic art, with singers looking and acting their parts. Ensemble action can be carefully planned and captured effectively by the camera. The essential details of the story can be brought out by means of well-prepared camera-shots, particularly close-ups. Opera in English can be exciting when good translations are used, especially with the microphone to help provide understandable enunciation. Realistic, three-dimensional scenery; lighting adapted to the requirements of the medium; proper make-up; technical devices like stills, dissolves, superimpositions and film-inserts—all these factors, used with skill and taste, can result in highly satisfactory television productions of opera.

Limitations of studio production But the telecasts also attest to the present deficiencies in studio production of opera, namely, the exclusion of Grand Operas like *Aida* or the *Ring*, due to the limitations of studio space; the anxiety to achieve realistic action with the tendency to cut purely musical standstills, such as overtures, contemplative arias and musical ensembles, which are nevertheless among the most valuable stylistic characteristics of opera; the lack of a solution to the problem of where to put the orchestra and how to achieve artistic co-ordination between conductor and singers; and finally, the absence of actual, live audience participation. A studio production which sacrifices this essential element of the theatrical experience in order to gain technical advantages forgets the fact that it cannot achieve the visual perfection of a film. Therefore it risks losing one of television's most valuable assets—its immediacy—without adequate gain.

Television has three decisive assets, however, which contribute greatly to democratic acceptance of opera: (*a*) the presentation of opera as realistic theatre; (*b*) the use of the language of the audience; and (*c*) last, but not least, the possibility of reaching an audience of enormous proportions. A sold-out Metropolitan performance, repeated eight times during ten years, would be seen and heard by about 250,000 people. One single telecast of the NBC Opera Company is witnessed by a nation-wide audience many times that large, running into the millions.

Besides studio performances there are other forms of TV production of opera which, though at present less conspicuous, are potentially extremely important. These are: (*a*) video transmission of opera from the actual performance in the opera house, already being practiced in Europe, as we saw; and (*b*) the production of operatic films.

Theatre telecasts

Television relay from the operatic stage was used to great effectiveness in America in the early years of the medium. On October 29, 1948, the American Broadcasting Company's Station WJZ-TV in New York transmitted the opening of the Metropolitan season, Verdi's *Otello*, to six cities along the Eastern seaboard. The Metropolitan opening performances of the successive two seasons, *Rosenkavalier* in 1949 and *Don Carlo* in 1950, were also televised.

In December, 1952, an important event took place when the complete Metropolitan production of *Carmen* was telecast on a closed circuit from the actual performance by a new enterprise, "Theatre Television." Three years later the mélange of four single acts from different operas which served as an opening performance for the 1955–56 season was presented in a similar way. "Theatre Television" transmitted the Metropolitan performances to thirty movie theatres across the nation. Many people in San Francisco or Denver dressed for the occasion, as though they were attending the Metropolitan opening in New York. These closed-circuit telecasts from the Metropolitan stage were abandoned because of unmanageable expenses. Now attempts are being made to establish pay-as-you-see television. These systems could become of great importance to opera by providing a paying audience.

Telecasts from actual performances in America suffer from the same technical shortcomings we noted in European transmissions. These include unfavorable camera positions, insufficient lighting and, in general, lack of proper technical preparation. Traditional acting, or rather lack of acting, physical unfitness of the singers, canvas scenery and poor costuming and make-up offer further obstacles. And yet, many of these shortcomings are compensated for by television's greatest asset—its ability to make the viewer feel that he is participating in an actual event that is happening *now*.

Operatic films

Operatic films, the third form of using opera on TV, have been limited so far to importations from abroad, such as the successful *Aida*, in which Sophia Loren acted the title role to the voice of Renata Tebaldi; the Japanese *Butterfly*; and Paul Czinner's documentary film of my production of *Don Giovanni* at the Salzburg Festival, mentioned previously. No professional operatic films have as yet been produced especially for TV, as far as I know. Various enterprises are under consideration, and kinescope films of NBC opera productions, such as those of Prokofieff's *War and Peace* and *Don Giovanni*, have been shown over European networks. Commercial calculations, however, seem so far to have discouraged the realization of operatic TV films.

Further progress in operatic telecasting required

Except for NBC's noble Opera Company, commercial television in America has not sponsored operatic TV productions comparable in any way to the output of the Italian, British, German or Austrian television systems, with their nation-wide, and, at times, continent-wide service, despite notable technical advances in the field of video tape and the financial resources of the competing American networks. Nor has the limited place allotted opera in programming favored progress in the planning of TV studios and theatres to accommodate operatic productions. The NBC Television City in Burbank, California, provides outstanding technical facilities; but the problems of a satisfactory placement of the orchestra and of contact between conductor and singers have not been solved. As in Europe, conductor and orchestra in American TV productions are frequently pushed into another room. This may make life more comfortable for the technicians, but it is less so for the composer and the audience. As far as I know, the new theatres presently in the planning stage or under construction make provision for proper cable contacts for TV cameras; but they do not aim basically at new approaches to TV transmission of opera.

With commercial television offering serious limitations to operatic programming and new production techniques, our eyes turn to the newest development in the TV field: the emergence of educational television.

Educational Television

As a result of the combined efforts of far-sighted educators and citizens, who organized a National Citizens Committee for Educational Television, the Federal Communications Commission in 1952 allocated 242 television channels for education. This number was later increased to 258. The Fund for Adult Education, established by the Ford Foundation in 1951, immediately took a decisive lead in helping local communities to organize educational stations. On May 25, 1953, the first station, KUHT in Houston, went on the air. Seven years later, more than fifty were in operation. The number is still increasing. Dean George D. Stoddard of New York University very accurately assessed television's significance to education when he called it "the greatest development in the art of communication since the invention of printing."

The growth of educational television is due in great measure to the interest and generous support given by the Ford Foundation and its associated funds. In 1952, the Educational Television and Radio Center, now the National Educational Television and Radio Center, was created by a grant from the Fund for Adult Education; it was later underwritten by the Ford Foundation to provide a national program service. The N.E.T.R.C. has become of outstanding importance in this field. In addition to its regular services, it sponsors the National Educational Television (N.E.T.) Film Service, as a joint project with the Audio-Visual Center of Indiana University in Bloomington, Indiana. This agency makes educational TV materials available to wide audiences on 16 mm. films. Under another program, Extended Services, educational programs are supplied for use over commercial television stations in communities without educational stations. More recently the N.E.T.R.C. was enabled by the Ford Foundation to supply the educational TV stations with the latest videotape equipment.

In 1959, John F. White, President of the N.E.T.R.C., predicted at a Conference in Washington that within five years the Center will be recognized as the fourth major TV network in the country. Considering this rapid development, it is hardly possible to overlook its implications for a non-commercial cultural form like opera, particularly if one considers the growth of opera departments at American universities and the initiation of public services in the field of music by educational stations like WGBH-TV, which has been carrying regular transmissions of the Boston Symphony concerts.

Pioneering advances into this new field are the occasional telecasts of opera produced by universities and transmitted by educational TV stations, and the film series "Spotlight on Opera," produced by the University Extension Division of the University of California. The recent move of the executive offices of N.E.T.R.C. from Ann Arbor, Michigan, to New York would seem to have particular significance. Their location on the same floor occupied by the executive staff of the Lincoln Center for the Performing Arts may be a good omen, not only for friendly relations but also for constructive common policies in the future.

Conclusions of Part II

In summary, these are the major factors which characterize opera in America:

1. Professional opera, unlike its counterpart in Europe, is not anchored solidly in the cultural tradition of America. Lacking the recognition opera receives in Europe, and the corresponding governmental subsidy, it has a very insecure artistic and economic existence.

2. This insecurity does not allow American opera to achieve either a consistent artistic policy nor modern standards of production.

3. Nevertheless, in recent years strong, new forces have been developing in America. These include new methods of sponsorship, a growing popularity of concert performances of operas by symphony orchestras, numerous projects for new theatres, the development of opera production in workshops and on television, in addition to growing public interest and an amazing wealth of operatic talent.

4. For these reasons, the mere imitation of European operatic traditions, either in organization, production or architecture, cannot solve the problem of producing professional opera in America. European opera should be carefully studied and the lessons learned applied judiciously to the situation as we find it in the United States.

Let us now try to propose a program for opera in America.

Part III. Producing Opera for America

Introduction: Opera and its Function within the American Community
(Some Basic Questions)

American production methods
for opera needed

We saw in Part I, *Opera in Europe*, and in Part II, *Opera in the United States*, that the social, economic and artistic conditions are entirely different on the two continents. In my opinion, the United States must develop its own approach to opera production, based on the situation as it exists in America. Before we proceed to concrete proposals, let us make some basic observations regarding the function of opera within the American community.

We must first of all reach a clear understanding of opera as an art form transplanted into the American community. There is no agreement as yet in America on even basic questions regarding opera.

Do we want primarily the musical *sound* in opera, or are we interested equally in the *word* motivating it? Should we aim to produce Grand Opera or musical theatre? Is it more important to have "stars," or an integral ensemble? Do we want to see the conductor, or should he and the orchestra be out of sight? Do we prefer the historic box-theatre, or a modern auditorium? Should the theatre be made small, for the few in top hat; or big, for the masses? Should we have traditional or streamlined staging? Government subsidy or self-supporting opera? What is opera: "entertainment," "education"—or something more?

Finding answers to these questions, and dozens of others like them, requires knowledge and courage. For in America, where the enthusiasm of both the dilettante and the professional are needed to achieve an operatic performance, we find that emotions and personal opinions, if not snobbery, often replace common sense and fact. Let us therefore take a straight-forward look at some of these questions.

154

Opera as "Entertainment"

Opera as a cultural possession

There are people in America who believe they do opera a favor by advertising it as "entertainment" or "amusement." Often they try to avoid the word "opera" completely, because they are afraid that the public will shy away from "highbrow" art. They underestimate both American audiences and the practical consequences of their attitude. The *Barber of Seville* and other operas ought to be good entertainment, but the term cannot very well be applied to *Tristan*, *Oedipus Rex* or *Susannah*. While there is no need to picture opera as a "long-hair" affair—such an idea was far from the minds of Mozart or Verdi—there is, on the other hand, no point either in considering opera a cultural expression inferior to the symphony or the fine arts. Nor are opera's spiritual and educational values something of which we must be ashamed. It is precisely this basic recognition of opera as a cultural possession that puts the opera house on a level with the symphony orchestra, the school and the museum, and thereby justifies its public support.

If opera is classified as entertainment, the citizen might properly expect—and he frequently does, in America—that it ought to make money the way commercial musicals, television shows and films do. As a matter of fact, several noble operatic endeavors have been started in the past with the help of sponsors, who left them when the company began to concentrate on "making money." One example is the former New Opera Company of New York, which turned from Verdi's *Macbeth*, with Fritz Busch as conductor, and *Così fan tutte*, to *Rosalinda*, and so down the road to productions with the most box-office appeal. America has supported generously not only religious and educational organizations, but also symphony orchestras and fine-arts museums. But it will not sponsor opera on the Pasternak-Melchior or Ed Sullivan-Helen Traubel formula, which is supposed to make its own money anyway. Only the recognition of opera as one of our civilization's greatest achievements—a non-commercial, cultural expression fully deserving of united community sponsorship—will make possible the kind of financial support this art must have for its future development.

Opera in English

Truth and consequences

Another basic problem, more closely connected with the preceding one than many might think, is the much-debated question of whether to sing opera in

155

English. Nobody will deny that opera in the original language sounds better than in a translation—especially if one is able to understand the original. There are also good reasons for Grand Opera companies to perform opera in the original languages, when their foreign singers are more convincing interpreters than those available otherwise. There is also no reason why a festival should not enjoy a guest performance by the Vienna Opera singing in German, or why a wealthy Maecenas should not transport an entire Italian opera house to his American estate for the benefit of his friends, if it pleases him and he can afford it. But why, otherwise, should opera in America, as in no other country, be denied the right to be understood by either the majority of its interpreters or its audience? I understand the answers to this question still less now, after twenty-five years of activity in America, than I did at first when I, as a newcomer, was told it was simply a question I couldn't understand. In my native Vienna it was the custom to present all foreign operas in translation. Toscanini conducted *Pelléas* in Italian for his countrymen in Milan, and in Munich Bruno Walter presented Verdi in German. Judging from listening to Purcell's and Handel's music, I cannot understand why English should not be singable, nor why bad enunciation of foreign opera in foreign languages by foreign or American artists is happily accepted in America. Finally, one day, I was given the answer by a charming lady—and her viewpoint is no rarety—"I do not want to understand the words," said she, "I want to understand the music."

Those who believe with me that the words must be understood, as Mozart, Verdi, Wagner and Richard Strauss insisted, take consolation in the fact that while the connoisseurs are debating the language question in theory, opera workshops and television producers have decided the problem, at least for themselves, in practice. They have demonstrated that common sense can be applied even to the production of opera.

Operatic Snobbery

The case of Van Cliburn

The "European complex" is not limited to the language question. The Sputnik-like musical career of Van Cliburn made it clearly evident that a Texas artist is both a better artist and a better box-office attraction when launched in Moscow rather than in Dallas. The time when Edward Johnson had to become Edoardo di Giovanni for a successful career in America is not completely past.

Just recently I engaged Virginia Copeland, an outstanding American soprano, under the name of "Gordoni."

After a professional life in the United States covering a quarter of a century, I know from personal experience that it is far easier to get the attention of the New York papers—and they *are* important for an artist's career in America—for a performance done in Europe rather than in America. For instance, I feel that my productions of Wagner's *Walküre* and the scenic presentation of Haydn's *Creation*, both at the Red Rocks Theatre near Denver, were of much greater significance than many of my European stagings. And yet it was much more difficult to obtain recognition for them in the United States.

This sort of snobbery makes the employment of operatic artists other than "name" singers difficult for both artists and managements. Instead of using the excellent young talent available, opera organizations even in smaller communities are forced to look for the Tebaldis and di Stefanos, even though artists of this reputation not only consume the major part of the available budget but frequently destroy the artistic ensemble because of their unavailability for rehearsals and the resulting lack of integration of the performance. In Europe, opera stages like those of Stockholm, Basle or Wuppertal would never have achieved high standards if they had depended on Milan or Vienna for their leading singers. The general use of American artists in American opera houses for leading roles would not, of course, exclude occasional guest appearances by famous foreign artists nor guest performances by the Metropolitan at the end of the season, to set standards for competition. But today it is as though guest appearances by the Philadelphia Orchestra were considered the only way to enjoy good symphonic music in Pittsburgh, whereas this city has been able to set high standards in the concert field through the excellent achievements of its own orchestra.

The same snobbery leads to support of European cultural activities by private American citizens at the expense of similar activities in the United States.

I certainly do not belong among those who complain that the reconstruction of the Vienna Opera and, among others, La Scala, was possible only because of the Marshall Plan, while American government support is not available for opera at home. The truth is that this money was generously made available by the United States for the recovery of Western European countries. It was the decision of the people in Vienna and Milan to use the money to restore their opera houses even before they rebuilt their own demolished homes. To these people the reconstruction of their opera houses seemed more important.

The " European complex"

More recently Menotti's Festival of Two Worlds in Spoleto, Italy, received generous American aid. I am glad to see the Spoleto Festival supported; yet it remains a strange fact that while an annual subsidy of about $150,000, including a considerable amount of American government and foundation money, was available for Spoleto, it seemed impossible to raise $25,000 for a summer festival in New Mexico or Colorado. And this despite the fact that at Denver about 30,000 people attended two performances each of *The Girl of the Golden West* and *The Creation* during July, 1959, defying wind and rain and showing an enthusiasm for opera that our American papers report of the opera-loving audiences in places like Verona, Italy.

Government Support

Growing interest in opera

The enormous growth of public interest in serious music, including opera, is what augurs best for the future. "Can statistics prove anything?" asked John Rosenfield in *The Dallas Morning News* of July 18, 1959, and answered as follows: "The final years of Federal amusement tax on opera and concerts showed that the patronage of highbrow music was the largest in the entertainment field, except that for motion pictures, of course . . . Attendance at concerts, operas, ballets, stage plays and other alleged preciosities of diversion exceeded by many millions that for all spectator sports, football and baseball included . . . Few unheeded observers argued, as we did, that grand opera didn't frighten people, only the cost ($8 and $10) of an opera ticket did. We were wasting manual energy at the typewriter."

To this we must add the fact that there are more than 727 opera-producing organizations in America, including 200 college workshops and an increasing number of orchestras presenting opera in concert form. There were a total of 4,000 opera performances in the United States during the season 1958–59.* Granted, many of these performances were far from professional, but the figure alone indicates the growing nation-wide interest in opera. This fact could not

* According to *Opera News*, November 14, 1959.

158

fail to stimulate sponsorship by private individuals, and has also resulted in increased recognition of opera by foundations and even by the government.

Support of educational and cultural activities by individuals and foundations is, in contrast to Europe, basic to the American tradition. More than seven billion dollars is contributed annually in the United States for religious, charitable and educational purposes. Business organizations are taking an increasingly greater interest in the support of higher education. "New foundations, both large and small, continue to appear on the scene; approximately 11,000 foundations combined represent a bit more than seven per cent of the total philanthropic effort. Something more than half of the seven-billion-dollar total is contributed for religious purposes; about a third goes to health and welfare services; and more than an eighth as private support for education."*

New patterns of support: Foundations

The burgeoning interest of the American public in the arts has been reflected in the new attitude of foundations toward the support of artistic endeavors. The first grants were awarded in the field of opera during the last decade. The Rockefeller Foundation *President's Review* of 1956 explained its motivation in making grants for the arts as follows:

"There are many reasons for believing that the role of the arts in American society is changing, that the changes are potentially for the better, and that new patterns of support for the arts may need to be pioneered in the United States.

"Throughout much of human history the support of the fine arts has come from a small fraction of the population endowed by birth, wealth, or ecclesiastical position with the means to provide patronage. In a modern democracy, and particularly in the United States, shifts in income distribution and the fluidity of the class structure have considerably decreased the economic importance of the wealthy while increasing that of middle and lower income groups. The small groups traditionally interested in the arts have in many instances lost both the power and the means to give them inspiration and support. The larger groups which have gained in economic strength and which might be expected to take the place of the patrons of the past have not always had active artistic interests nor convenient methods for pooling individual small contributions . . .

* From *The President's Review*, Annual Report of the Rockefeller Foundation, 1958.

"Although there are many reasons to believe that the future of the arts in a modern society is a bright one, the patterns of artistic activity—and particularly social and financial support of art—must keep pace with the larger economic and social changes if that future is to be realized. The serious economic difficulties which still confront the arts and artists arise largely from the facts that our aspirations steadily exceed our expanding capabilities and that we are evolving from outmoded and inadequate forms of organization and support to new and, it is hoped, better ones."

This change of attitude with regard to the arts was not limited to the Rockefeller Foundation. In 1957, the Ford Foundation enlarged its previous project in the Humanities, combining it with a new Creative Arts Program. Explaining this step, the Foundation stated, "Many people believe that a re-examination of the traditional ways by which cultural institutions have been organized and given financial support is required." This Program for the Humanities and the Arts has become of far-reaching importance in the development of opera and theatre building. Both the Rockefeller and Ford Foundation grants, however, are made not as contributions toward the regular operating expenses of any organization, but for the creative development of artists and program ideas.

Government recognition Growing public concern with the arts, which was reflected in the new philosophy adopted by foundations, could not but result also in various endeavors to promote government recognition and subsidy for the arts, including opera. The American National Theatre and Academy (ANTA), chartered by an act of Congress in 1935, has been of vast and varied practical service to the government and the people ever since. This charter is unique in the arts, however.

Over the years a number of bills have been presented to Congress in behalf of sponsorship of the arts. Among them were several to establish "A National Theatre and a National Opera and Ballet" (Resolution by Senators Jacob K. Javits and Irving M. Ives of New York, 1949); a "Fine Arts Programs in Colleges Bill" (Representative Charles R. Howell, 1952); five bills to create the long-awaited Federal Advisory Council on the Arts; and a United States Arts Foundation Bill (Senators Javits and Clark, 1959).

The Javits and Clark Bill, proposing a United States Arts Foundation, seeks to provide "national recognition of the status of the theatre and other performing arts as a cherished and valued part of the Nation's cultural resources since

160

colonial days." The Foundation would be directed by a board of trustees appointed by the President. "The President shall endeavor to provide representation to the several performing arts, to both civic, educational and professional groups concerned with and engaged in productions of the performing arts, to the trade unions and trade associations concerned with the performing arts, and to the attending public." And it proposes to provide to professional and educational groups in this field, "through direct grant or otherwise, financial assistance and support from the funds appropriated to the Foundation or otherwise obtained pursuant to this Act or other Acts," adding that "the Foundation shall wherever practicable develop the principle of matching funds with interested agencies public or private."*

Combined sponsorship

While the establishment of such a Federal Advisory Council on the Arts, or a United States Arts Foundation, is unquestionably of the utmost importance to provide official recognition of and practical assistance to the arts, it would seem to me to be even more important to establish civic and state arts foundations as well; for these would be in a better position to understand the problems of a particular community, county and state. At the same time they would have closer contact with and be better able to solicit the local sponsorship of individuals and foundations. The participation of government and private sponsorship would have value not only in terms of financial contributions, but also in terms of personal interest and a sense of personal obligation. A collaboration of this kind between official government agencies, national, state and local, and private organizations and individuals, seems to me the most practical path that sponsorship can take in the American community.

The American Production Elements

Co-operation between individual groups is needed

It cannot be denied that co-operation between the various arts within the American community is often hard to achieve. Personal interests frequently block the common good. Mrs. A., president of the local symphony association, does not wish to compromise her own status or that of her group in reaching any agreement with the community opera company, whose chairman, Mrs. B.,

---

* Quotations from *Bill S. 1598, to establish the United States Arts Foundation*, introduced in the Senate on April 7, 1959.

161

probably has similar feelings, even though several directors serve on the boards of both institutions. The leaders of the museum group may feel the same way about working with the music school, which in turn does not want to collaborate with the local opera workshop.

In Colorado, the Central City Opera Board cannot reach a hand toward the Red Rocks Festival, although the operatic repertory of each group, one having a theatre seating 700, the other, 9,000, would be completely different. An integrated policy would provide much greater attractions for audiences coming from afar to this region. Recently in New York, the Metropolitan Opera, the City Center Opera and the NBC Opera Company were all presenting *Così fan tutte* in English in independent productions. Conceivably one opera company and the NBC Network could have joined forces, while the third company produced a different work.

In general, symphony orchestras in America are supported without sharing in opera and light opera productions, even though their own house is frequently an opera house (as, for instance, in Philadelphia), or is from time to time used for opera (as in Pittsburgh, Kansas City, Denver, etc.). Can America really afford this waste and duplication of talent and financial resources by separating the musical groups at a time when each one, individually, is pleading for assistance? It seems obvious that not division, but rather co-operation between the arts is essential to secure their artistic and economic existence and in particular to make possible the production of opera within the American community.

Co-operation between the arts, and a unified, organized sponsorship, are the two basic requisites for the secure existence of opera in America. The systematic encouragement and exploitation of the vital forces we recognized as developing on the American operatic scene are equally important. Day-dreaming about the traditional million-dollar subsidies of Vienna or Milan will do little good. But exploring patiently the most promising ideas, and promoting enthusiastically the organizations which have developed out of conditions peculiar to the American community, will show American opera the way. These include:

1. United community sponsorship of opera companies *and* symphony orchestras.
2. Acceptance of new approaches to theatre building.
3. Development of indigenous artistic policies.

4. Collaboration of professional companies with opera schools and workshops.

5. Exploitation of commercial and educational television.

These elements must form the building material for the American opera company of the future.

I. Projects in the Making

Opera at Lincoln Center

A new concept: Arts Center Both the increasing public interest in the arts and the obvious desirability of bringing them together resulted recently in a new and promising concept, uniquely American: the establishment of arts centers.

On May 14, 1959, when President Eisenhower broke ground for the Lincoln Center for the Performing Arts in New York, this extraordinary cultural project reached the stage of realization after three years of planning. For the first time in history opera, symphony, drama, operetta, dance, music school, museum and library are to be allied in one cultural complex. In 1956, the President of Lincoln Center, John D. Rockefeller 3rd, defined it as "a symbol of American cultural maturity, affirming for people everywhere our faith in the life of the spirit." The project was an exemplary evidence of American civic spirit. The individual arts groups involved, operating as private projects with private sponsorship, worked together with the city and federal governments toward final realization of the undertaking.

Government and private sponsorship Title I of the National Housing Act provides that American cities can ask for financial assistance from the federal government in condemnation of slum areas. These areas are bought at a fair price and turned over to approved private developers. The loss incurred in this procedure is carried two-thirds by the federal government and one-third by the city. This assistance enabled Lincoln Center to acquire land and to start demolition proceedings on a huge site covering three and one-half blocks in West Manhattan between 62nd and 66th Streets, bounded on either side by Columbus and Amsterdam Avenues and Broadway. This area formerly contained 2,030 tenants in 188 buildings.

Generous pledges from individuals and foundations made possible the start of the $130,000,000 project. There were grants of more than ten million dollars each from both the Rockefeller and Ford Foundations. Other private contributions have been substantial. These include a three-million-dollar gift from Mrs. V. Beaumont Allen to build a Repertory Theatre. By the fall of 1960, nearly $66,000,000 of the $102,000,000 goal had been raised from public donations. In the total budget, education has not been neglected; a ten-million-dollar fund has been earmarked for "educational aid and for fostering creative artistic advancement."

The buildings

Buildings are to include a new theatre for the Metropolitan Opera, with a seating capacity of 3,800; the Philharmonic Hall, with 2,600 seats; a theatre for dance and operetta, seating 2,500, with a Band Shell for open-air concerts on the west; the Juilliard School, with a theatre seating 900 and a chamber music and recital hall for 600; the Repertory Drama Theatre, seating 1,100; and the Library-Museum. The latter is expected to be under the guidance of the New York Public Library.

Wallace K. Harrison, the chief architect of the entire project, will be responsible for the Metropolitan Opera, his partner Max Abramovitz for the Philharmonic Hall, Philip Johnson for the Dance Theatre, and Pietro Belluschi for the Juilliard School. Eero Saarinen, with Joe Mielziner as collaborating designer, will plan the Drama Theatre, and Skidmore, Owings and Merril the Library-Museum. The theatre architects are being assisted by a group of outstanding experts in various fields. Those engaged so far include Walter Unruh for stage technics; Ben Schlanger for seating; Bolt, Beranek & Newman, Hope Bagenal and Werner Gabler for acoustics. The undertaking is obviously enormous.

New artistic planning required

Important as architectural planning is, the Center also expects the artistic planning to match the physical concept. The President of the Rockefeller Foundation stated in his *Annual Report* of 1957, "The Foundation's activity in the humanities, as in its other fields of interest, has never centered on buildings. Brick and mortar are necessary ingredients in the establishment of strong institutions in whatever field, but the dynamic functioning of the institution is the important thing which the Foundation seeks to support. In the arts the Foundation's aim is to encourage the flow of creativity which alone can bring innovation and change on the one hand and the perfection and strengthening of vital traditions on the other. The Lincoln Center project does not solve all the problems of encouraging creativity in the performing arts. But the interplay of related arts at the Center and the associated educational work may well offer a unique stimulus to creative development."

Opera at Lincoln Center is represented in four and, in a wider sense, five spheres: at the Metropolitan; at the Dance Theatre, in which it appears that not only the New York City Ballet but also the Opera Company of the New York City Center may become established; and at the Juilliard School, the Museum-Library and the Philharmonic Hall. The important question now is whether the constituent artistic organizations will continue their independent policies as before or will succeed in co-ordinating their activities for the common good. It would seem that constructive collaboration and planning is not only feasible but will, in the end, best serve the interests of the individual organizations.

The Metropolitan

The establishment of the new Metropolitan at Lincoln Center marks the end of a twenty-five-year period of democratic transition, during which America's historic home of international opera evolved from an opera house for the relative few into a national institution.

The old "Met"

Long ago it became evident, however, that the old Metropolitan building had serious drawbacks, despite its cherished historic auditorium and its fine acoustics. Various members of the audience found their view of the stage limited by poor sightlines. Totally outmoded production facilities made modern staging difficult, if not impossible. Lack of storage space, with make-shift storage arrangements in distant warehouses and rising costs of transportation, cut heavily into the budget. In a repertory theatre, where productions change every day and night, this was a matter for growing concern.

Unfortunately, the basic design of the old theatre and its physical location made it impossible to overcome these difficulties. A modern opera house was required, which would combine the best of American architectural concepts with the most advanced technical design and equipment.

The new look

The plans for the new Metropolitan reflect this thinking. Much attention has been given to the basic problem of sightlines and acoustics. Public areas and accommodations will be attractive. A modern stage with a flexible proscenium, two side stages, and one back stage carrying a revolving table, as well as modern lighting equipment, will make possible up-to-date productions. For the millions of Americans who will attend these performances through the mediums of radio and television, proper provisions have been made for the handling of microphones and television cameras. There will be rooms in which to construct, paint and store scenery, costumes, properties and wigs. There will be modern rehearsal halls, dressing rooms and sufficient office space. Air conditioning will make the house usable on a year-round basis. The new Metropolitan will incorporate, in building design and operating facilities, the best features of the new European opera houses.

The Met's tradition

Basically, the Met's policy is clearly defined by its tradition as America's historic theatre of international Grand Opera. This, however, carries with it a responsibility to improve its productions and its operation. In the light of increased public demand for tickets, it is essential that it make a careful analysis of its difficult and costly repertory system and, in that connection, its subscription system, with a view to possible revision. Reduction of the number of operas given in any one week and the period during which any opera is kept in the repertory are basic problems which involve artistic quality. The solution of these questions, in turn, will make it possible to keep intact the ensemble, as well as lower the cost of "stars." Let us hope that the modernized stage will be used to simplify production in line with modern concepts, utilizing quick shifts of scenery, rather than to submerge the opera and the singing actor in technical tricks. May we suggest that productions can be conceived in such a way that they will permit satisfactory telecasts from actual performances, as well as making possible their further use for filming during off-season months. In short, we ask that the new Metropolitan evolve an artistic policy which represents not a fundamental change, but rather a modernization and stream-lining of its own historic tradition.

Joining the other arts and educational organizations

At Lincoln Center the Metropolitan will give up its "splendid isolation" of former days, as a more or less private cultural enterprise within the American community; it will now join forces with its sister arts—symphony, ballet and drama—and participate in the important field of educational training. The new Metropolitan will not merely be a successful old organization transplanted into a new building. Rather it will meet a clear new challenge and perform a double function: On the one hand, it will maintain and fortify its position as the nation's greatest opera organization, preserving the most vital historic traditions of

166

international Grand Opera with modern production techniques. On the other, it will help create the opera of the future.

America's Opéra comique

Its function

It is obvious that there are many important possibilities in the field of opera that the Metropolitan, devoted to its own task, cannot hope to exploit in a comprehensive way: the presentation of an *opéra comique* repertory, ranging from seventeenth century operas to modern American works; the development of new operatic artists; experimentation with new scenic techniques; the cultivation of opera in English; the presentation of light opera and musical comedy; and experimentation with television studio production, particularly in connection with educational telecasting and taping. Obviously there is need for an organization supplementing the artistic program of the Metropolitan just as the Opéra Comique supplements the Opéra in Paris, the Volksoper the Staatsoper in Vienna, and Sadlers Wells the Covent Garden Opera in London.

Definition of program is important

In the past, this program has been carried out in part by the New York City Center Company. Unfortunately, whether as a result of personality clashes or financial necessity, there has been a lack of collaboration with the Metropolitan, and the City Center has had no clear definition of program. This has frequently resulted in a duplication of efforts. There was certainly no necessity for both organizations to compete in staging *Die Meistersinger* in German and *Macbeth* in Italian, nor was there much sense in the previously-mentioned independent productions of *Così fan tutte* by the Met, the City Center and the NBC Opera Company, all of which for the most part employed American artists singing in English.

Co-ordination with the Metropolitan Opera

If co-ordination between the two companies were achieved, the new American Opera Company could benefit the Metropolitan's interest enormously by developing and making available a group of young artists, who would then not have to be carried on the roster of the Metropolitan just to sing Annina in *La Traviata* and Ruiz in *Il Trovatore*, or be compelled to go to Europe to find a career. And it would do an equal service to opera by assuming the production of new, untried works, while modern works which have established their value, like *Wozzeck*, would be added to the Met repertory. Undoubtedly the younger company would also adopt performance in English as its definitive policy, and would act as a clearing-house for new talent not only for the Met, but for civic opera companies throughout the country.

Having a gifted personnel of young singers able to sing in English, the new company would also be well-equipped to assume the production of light opera and musical comedy. This could help close the gap which still exists between opera and musical theatre in America; and at the same time it would broaden the stage experience of the young artists—and the length of their contracts. Finally, this company, since it would require the same type of good-looking, versatile young artists as are presently employed by the NBC Opera Company, could join forces with television for the benefit of both groups.

Artistic policy

Not depending on a subscription system like the Metropolitan, the American Opéra comique could develop its own artistic policy, based on the principle of fewer works repeated more often during a longer period. These should be staged in a modern, simple way. I would advocate a new approach: a series of productions conceived from the outset for use and amortization in live performance, studio telecast and filming or taping for use on educational television programs.

Since this company would co-ordinate its activities with the ballet company in staging light operas, musical comedies and TV productions, the length of its season could be extended, possibly into a year-round activity. Artists could then live without "star" fees. The total budget would not be excessive and could be met if contributions from private individuals and foundations were continued as at present, and additional income from commercial television as well as from rapidly-expanding educational television could be expected.

The new theatre

It is evident that the projected Dance and Operetta Theatre being designed by Philip Johnson would furnish a logical home for this American Opera Company. Whether or not this company evolves out of the present New York City Center Opera, as one would expect after the important spadework that the City Center group has done in this field, or whether it will be installed at Lincoln Center in another form, the establishment of the new company requires close collaboration with the Metropolitan.

Assuming this project materializes, the planners of the Dance and Operetta Theatre will necessarily consider the layout and technical equipment of the stage in the light of the production requirements of such a program. In this

168

theatre, where tradition would not be involved to the same extent as at the Metropolitan, there should be greater freedom for the realization of new and exciting American ideas.

A model for the entire country   Such an opera company, established in a new theatre, collaborating with and supplementing the activities of the Metropolitan Opera in line with a clearly defined policy, will be of importance not only for the Metropolitan Opera and New York City, but will serve also as a model for the establishment of more community opera companies throughout the nation. It will, together with the Metropolitan as the modernized home of Grand Opera, make an important creative contribution toward the development of opera in America.

Educational Plans

Interrelationship between performing arts and education   Just as the founding of Lincoln Center makes possible an alliance between Grand Opera and the American version of *opéra comique* or folk opera, it opens the way for constructive interrelationships between professional opera companies and educational organizations. Fortunately, the Lincoln Center project stressed from the beginning its great interest in education, as noted above, and earmarked generous funds for this purpose. The Rockefeller Foundation alone indicated that a quarter of its $10,050,000 grant would be used for "scholarships and artistic development in music, the dance and drama."

Policy of artistic integration   Nothing is more important for the future of opera in the United States, particularly the development of operatic talent, than a living interchange between the teaching, performing artist of outstanding quality and the highly-gifted advanced student. It will be possible to achieve this at Lincoln Center. Here again, however, we face the problem of established privilege. The Juilliard School of Music has its Opera Department and the Metropolitan has its Kathryn Long classes. The City Center, the Metropolitan and Juilliard all have their own ballet schools, etc. The question is whether this duplication should continue, or whether there should be a policy of integration. It would be a tragic loss and a betrayal of mission if Lincoln Center turns out to be merely an accumulation of the same old independent organizations doing business in the same old way in a new location. It would be just as unfortunate, however, if these organizations were to go into direct competition with the many excellent music schools scattered throughout the United States.

Lincoln Center, as I see it, should draw from the entire country—and the world—the best material available for *final professional training*. The United States has many elementary music schools. What it does *not* have, and needs desperately, is an advanced educational center where America's finest talent can achieve final polish through contact with professional performers and performances, as is today provided in Europe, to a certain degree, by the smaller theatres.

In America an attempt in this direction is being made by opera workshops and small opera groups of various kinds, but it must be admitted in all honesty that these groups often lack both teachers of high professional standards and, as in most of the university workshops, students of outstanding qualifications, since the students are in most cases admitted to receive a general musical education rather than professional training.

Dr. Sergei Koussevitzky, feeling this lack of final professional education, conceived the idea of the Berkshire Music Center. The Center was originally designed to offer performing courses for orchestra players, conductors, composers and choir singers. Following my suggestion, Dr. Koussevitzky added an Opera Department to the curriculum of the school. Despite many positive results, two shortcomings of this school soon became evident: The six-week school session was not sufficient to realize fully the professional goals; and the admission of too many students, some without the necessary qualifications, did not tend to ensure professional results.

As we noted earlier, the close collaboration between conservatory and professional opera company, which once existed in Europe during the classic period of the conservatories at Naples and Paris, is now a thing of the past. But even today there is still a practical, working relationship between several leading opera houses and ballet companies and carefully selected students. In Italy we noted earlier the Opera School of La Scala (in addition to the Conservatory of Music) in Milan; the opera course at Spoleto, sponsored by the Rome Opera; and the Centro Lirico in Florence. Sweden has an Opera School associated with the Opera at Stockholm, and at Zurich an international opera studio is being established in collaboration with the Stadttheater.

In America, however, such opportunities are harder to find. It is true that there are the Metropolitan's Kathryn Long classes, the City Center program, the San Francisco Opera Company's summer training program, and Santa Fé's new opera school, but comprehensive collaboration between opera training schools and professional opera companies is still lacking. Considering the realities of professional opera in the United States, as well as the unique chance Lincoln Center will have to bring together for the first time *all* the performing arts *and* the young performing artists, I feel that a new educational project should be developed.

An Advanced Academy for the Performing Arts advocated

I suggest, therefore, that Lincoln Center should act also as an Educational Center for the Performing Arts. The Juilliard School of Music should, in my opinion, quite aside from its own basic training of opera singers, establish an *Advanced Academy for the Performing Arts*, with an *Opera Division*. The participants in this Academy should be selected from among the best young operatic artists available, whether discovered in music schools or studying under private teachers. Talent should be invited both from the United States and from the world at large. When the Academy discovered an exceptional talent without previous training, it should consider placing the student for elementary training in Juilliard's own school or with some private teacher of its confidence, but this student should not be admitted to the Academy roster until thoroughly trained and ready for acceptance on a competitive basis. Outstanding composers, librettists, singers, conductors, directors, choreographers, designers, coaches and stage-technicians who are actively engaged professionally at Lincoln Center theatres should be the teachers at the Advanced Academy.

The Academy participants should be admitted automatically to rehearsals and performances of every type presented at Lincoln Center. These participants should be furnished the widest possible training in the performing arts; an opera singer, for example, would not only be offered practical experience in operatic interpretation, but would participate in speech, drama and dance activities as well. Similar practical experience in related arts should be made available for the actor, the dancer, etc.

The new Juilliard Theatre

Most of the work should be achieved through preparation for actual performance in the Juilliard Theatre. This theatre should be designed in such a manner that it will make possible every conceivable approach to performance, ranging from traditional proscenium-type presentations to theatre in-the-round and experimental productions of a more novel sort. The theatre should also have facilities for TV transmissions, film-making and videotape recording. It is obviously of the greatest importance that the designers of such a flexible theatre should be inspired by the most modern concepts. New projects in Europe should be examined carefully and their best characteristics combined with the most advanced American ideas.

A Study Center of Operatic Production

Museum-Library

The Juilliard Advanced Academy should offer opportunities to study opera in every aspect of performance. This should not be limited to current productions, but should include historical study of all important past performances as well. Such a program can be realized only by the establishment of a *Study Center of Operatic Production*, set up in collaboration with the planned Museum-Library.

Here at the Study Center of Operatic Production a student interested in the interpretation of a particular opera would be able to see how it had been interpreted in the past, from the original première until the present day. Stage models, photographs, reviews in newspapers and periodicals, recordings and films, as well as books and scores, would be catalogued and available for rapid reference. A young stage director, designer, singer or critic interested in Wagner's *Walküre*, for instance, would be able to study not only Wagner's own original staging, but also later productions at Bayreuth, Appia's projects, and all other important scenic solutions from Alfred Roller to current presentations. As a constant source of information for participants in the Academy, such a Study Center would offer unique opportunities for the training in depth of the young operatic artist. It would also provide an opportunity to broaden public knowledge of and interest in opera, by providing television with comprehensive operatic source material.

In these ways, Lincoln Center can open up new horizons in the field of education, both for the artist and the public, and ultimately help achieve new standards for opera in America and the world.

Opera and Symphony

But opera is related to all the arts at Lincoln Center. Aside from its interest in the Repertory Drama program, it considers the symphony also an allied art, not only because of the participation of opera singers in concert performances of operas and oratorios, but also in view of a more recent development—the

172

staging of choral works, whether oratorios or contemporary compositions of a related type.

Staging of oratorios Today's audiences, influenced by film, television and news magazines, are becoming more visual-minded than before. At the same time, there is a growing tendency to present performances not only on proscenium stages, but also in concert halls with simple elements of staging. Works like Strawinsky's *Oedipus rex* and Milhaud's *Christophe Colombe* or *Roi David*, do not require a technically complicated conventional stage, but are equally effective, or even more so, when presented in an auditorium with simple facilities and without curtain.

This is true also in the staging of Handel oratorios—long since a custom in Europe. In 1959, in the auditorium at Indiana University, I presented Handel's *Belshazzar* in a successful staged version. Haydn's *Creation*, in a scenic presentation, was most enthusiastically received when produced at Red Rocks by the Denver Symphony Society during two successive seasons. The staging of Bach's *St. Matthew Passion*, long since advocated by progressive artists like Gordon Craig and Ferruccio Busoni, was first done in the United States by the team of Stokowski, Robert Shaw, Balanchine and Robert Edmond Jones in a New York presentation (1943); and by this author in Montreal, Canada (1943); as well as in Palermo, Sicily (1960). Mendelssohn's *Elijah* and other Handel oratorios open up new possibilities for staging by symphony and choral societies.

In view of these developments, it would be highly desirable to have the stage of the new Philharmonic Hall equipped not only with elevator platforms and a removable cyclorama for projections, but also proper lighting equipment. These provisions would involve relatively small additional expense, considering the fact that the Hall would then be usable not only for concerts, but also for the production of scenic oratorios and ballets.

Lincoln Center is a concrete expression of the growing recognition the performing arts are achieving within the American community, and of the American awareness of their interrelationship. The recent realization or planning of similar arts centers at several other strategic cultural points in the United States is proof that this concept is not limited to New York.

A Music Center for Los Angeles For example, after ten years of endeavor Los Angeles is about to break ground for a multi-purpose Music Center building, located in the heart of the city. This will supply a home for symphony, opera, light opera, musical comedy and ballet. Three times the public had turned down a bond issue to finance the Center. Collaboration between county government and private sponsors, under the chairmanship of Dorothy B. Chandler, finally accomplished the raising of the first ten million dollars. This made possible the start of the building by the architectural firm of Welton Becket and Associates. The house, seating 3,100, will have a modern stage and no boxes. It is hoped that the Music Center will be only the first of several buildings dedicated to the arts.

A National Cultural Center for Washington, D.C.

On September 2, 1958, Congress authorized a National Cultural Center to be established by private funds in Washington, D.C., to "present classical and contemporary music, opera, drama, dance and poetry from this and other countries," as well as to develop educational and other civic activities. The gigantic building on the Potomac River will, when architect Edward D. Stone's plans are realized, combine under one roof an opera house, a concert hall, a theatre, two smaller auditoriums and reception rooms.

A simpler scheme needed for other communities

But the performing arts in the United States, opera included, do not depend on the existence of gigantic arts centers in New York and Washington. Nor are the requirements of these great cities necessarily the same as those of other American communities. Many of the smaller cities could hardly support one opera company and a symphony orchestra in separate buildings. They need a far simpler scheme, in which opera would find its proper place. I will now attempt to make concrete proposals for these communities.

II. *The American Opera Company of the Future*

1. SPONSORSHIP

The local elements

When we take stock of the elements necessary for an operatic production which already exist within the American community, we see that there is a symphony orchestra, a choir, a struggling opera group, a dance school, a music school at the conservatory or university, an opera workshop, a theatre group, a fine arts organization and a television station, and there is also a theatre or auditorium. So, actually, all the ingredients needed for an operatic production are at hand— except money.

174

It is true that some of these elements, particularly the opera group and the theatre, may not be everything we dreamed. Others, like the music school and fine arts museum, are more solidly established. The most important group is the local symphony orchestra, and this has probably already achieved recognition and an established policy of sponsorship. Considering the fact that an orchestra is the most expensive part of a full-scale operatic performance, and that opera must be built up gradually and therefore cannot easily undertake the burden of creating a new orchestra, it is only natural that we turn first to the symphony organization to discuss the possibility of collaboration.

Collaboration with the symphony organization

We know that some of the leading board members and subscribers look down a bit on opera, but we also know that the musical director was formerly an opera conductor and at least once every season presents an opera in concert form. That is true of most of the leading symphony conductors, such as Reiner, Szell, Steinberg, Solti, Abravanel, Rudolf, Krips and others. We know too that the director is looking for new attractions besides modern symphonic compositions, which rarely fill his concerts, and wonders how long he will be able to schedule time and again the Brahms *Second* and Beethoven *Fifth*. And finally, we remember the short-season contracts of the orchestra players, who must undertake arduous tours in order to extend the number of their services and thus their paychecks.

We talk to the musical director and discuss with him the idea of replacing the concert performance of an opera with a staged version. He agrees to explore the idea. In a conference including our stage director, who is connected with the university opera or drama group and the local opera company, and the manager of the symphony orchestra, we decide on which operas the symphony would like to play and which, among these, would not require too complicated a staging. Then we proceed to make an estimate of the additional expense involved for the visual part of the production and the necessary rehearsals. If we agree upon doing one or two operas as part of the regular concert subscription series with as many (one or two) repeat performances as are done of each concert program, we find out to our surprise that the additional expense for the staging, above the expense of a concert performance, will be approximately between $7,500 and $12,500 per performance, or $30,000 to $50,000 for two or three performances of two operas.

We are fortunate that the symphony happens to play its concerts in a theatre;

175

otherwise we would have a difficult time with our proposal. The additional expense causes some hesitation at first. Positive factors soon gain the upper hand, however: the novel appeal of opera as part of the program series, the possibility of getting some financial return from a third student performance and from television transmission and, last but not least, the outlook of prolonging the orchestra season by two weeks. For the manager quickly recognizes the advantages of presenting one opera at the beginning and the other at the end of the concert season, thereby getting the season off to an exciting start and later giving it a stimulant at the time when general interest is slackening. The opera director points out the possibility of further development in the future. A third opera could be added in mid-season, the way the Utah Symphony presents a successful ballet week at Christmas. Over a martini the visions of the artists get more excited. Why not expand the fall, mid-season and spring opera schedules into short opera seasons including more works? Why not think about eventual integration of opera and symphony?

The business manager begs the artists to keep their heads cool and their feet on the ground. Presenting one or two operas at first, as part of the regular concert series, seems a feasible proposition. He agrees that if the season's subscribers are offered twelve concerts and two operas in place of the present fourteen concerts, they will not turn their tickets back but rather will be grateful for the new program. Yes, many tired businessman might find *Carmen* even more attractive than a Bach *Passion*.

Of course, there are problems to be solved. Should the symphony act as producer of the operas? Or should symphony and opera collaborate in the project? Should the musical director of the symphony conduct the operas or should the present musical director of the opera company be in charge of these performances? The problems and their solutions will be different in each community. The main question, however, "Can symphony and opera join forces for the common good?" finds an unqualified answer: "Yes!"

Now the proposal can be brought to the board of the symphony and its auxiliary committees, which have to decide whether to take on the production of opera under their own responsibility. They appoint a subcommittee for the supervision and promotion of the opera program. If only two or three operas are produced by the symphony, no great problems will arise, provided a capable stage director is invited to join the musical director and business manager. The estimated amount of about $15,000 to $25,000 for two or three performances of one opera lies within and even below the amount which American community opera companies are spending at present for such programs. Additional sponsorship from educational funds and television might further reduce the relatively modest expense. But if the next step, expansion of the operatic program, is to be undertaken, the task will be more complex.

The first question will be whether the symphony organization will produce the fall, mid-season and spring operas; or even whether full integration of opera and symphony is possible. When an established opera company exists in the community, the question may be whether the symphony should collaborate with it, providing only the services of the orchestra. In either case, the budget will rise in accordance with the expansion of the operatic program, and existing approaches to sponsorship will not be adequate.

Support of symphony and opera is severely limited in many communities because sponsors are divided into two competing groups; similarly, music schools, dance organizations and fine arts activities find themselves fighting for attention. A citizen who is interested in the symphony may not particularly want to support opera or the fine arts, and vice-versa. But while one can well imagine that a citizen might hesitate to contribute to more than one particular art form, he finds it difficult to deny his support to the arts as such.

United Arts Fund and Council For this reason a *United Arts Fund*, operating along the lines of the successful Cincinnati model, would be the most promising solution for community support of all the arts, including opera. It should be preceded by and combined with a civic *United Arts Council*, in which the interests of all the arts groups within the community are represented. The Council should include leaders of all the constituent organizations: the symphony, opera and light opera, dance, drama, school of the performing arts and fine arts groups. It should be headed by a widely-respected personality, such as the Mayor, the President of the University, or another substantial cultural leader of the community. It should also include representatives of the local educational institutions, local and regional foundations and business firms, as well as radio and television companies.

The organization of such an Arts Council would vary in each community. The best approach, in keeping with American tradition, would be to create an alliance of civic groups to exploit the possibilities of sponsorship by private individuals. A fund-raising committee of experts will find new ways to encourage the widest possible participation. American communities may find that the slogan, "A Dollar A Year For The Arts," will not remain unheeded. Such a campaign could raise a substantial amount in individual contributions; and if this sum were to be matched by local and regional foundations and business firms, the Arts Fund would be in a position to contribute decisively to the financing of the various performing and fine arts groups concerned. The aggregate amount, including possible revenues from educational and commercial sources might well be a figure comparable to the average annual civic subsidy granted by a German city to its symphony and theatres; namely, $1.43 per capita, or approximately $750,000, in a city of 500,000.

Government support When public interest has been stimulated, we can proceed gradually to add government to private support. State universities are even now offering civic assistance to the arts. We noted in the case of the Utah Symphony how university sponsorship can be of basic importance in the development of symphony, opera, light opera, dance and drama; and we remember the financial assistance given by Los Angeles County to opera produced for the schools. One step farther and we reach the point where a civic theatre is provided tax-free, or at a token fee, to the operating company, as happened in the case of the New York City Center. Still more significant is the practical assistance given by the federal and city governments toward realization of the arts center projects in New York and Washington.

Our proposed United Arts Council and Fund would accept private contributions from individuals, foundations and business firms; money or other assistance from commercial and educational resources; and support by the state or federal government. As far as government support is concerned, we are not advocating that it shoulder the whole load. And we are not afraid of serious interference by American politicians in artistic matters, an argument one hears frequently. (Has the Maecenas of the arts, whether emperor, Church or modern trustee, never exercised a bit of influence in return for generosity?)

Federal assistance, outside the Washington Arts Center project, can be more important at the moment in supplying official recognition and general encouragement to the arts, rather than providing actual funds, considering the huge size

178

of the country and the variety of its artistic programs. State, county and particularly city support would appear to be the best form of government subsidy in the United States, since local authorities can best judge the merits and possibilities of projects within their areas. Local government representatives, recognizing the importance of the arts for their own citizens, are also in a strategic position to make the most important and indispensable contribution—civic buildings with the necessary facilities. These could be put at the disposal of non-commercial art groups, including the local symphony and opera organization, free of charge.

2. THE NEW THEATRE

Civic Arts Centers

The present status of opera in America, outside of New York City, does not justify the expectation that most other cities might or should, with public funds, build a theatre devoted entirely to opera. Even theatres similar to San Francisco's War Memorial Opera House, which is used for opera, symphony and conferences, will lie beyond the realistic reach of most American communities. But a building suitable for symphony, opera, light opera and musical comedy, ballet and drama, as well as social and political functions—in short, a year-round *Civic Arts Center*—is an entirely feasible proposition for every larger American city. It is, in fact, a necessity.

Almost everywhere in the United States plans are now being discussed for the erection of new auditoriums, concert halls and theatres. It seems timely to put in an urgent plea that the requirements of opera and the other performing arts be studied carefully in the designing of these buildings. For most American cities I would personally recommend consideration of a new type of all-purpose building, which would include proper facilities for the presentation of opera, even in preference to theatres designed exclusively for opera.

The character of an Arts Center project would depend, of course, on the size and cultural demands of each particular city. Larger cities may require a larger hall, with 2,400 to 2,800 seats, for symphony, Grand Opera and meetings of various kinds; a smaller hall seating about 1,200 to 1,400, for legitimate drama and musicals; and a studio-recital hall accommodating about 600 to 700. In

179

smaller cities the Center should consist only of one large hall and a small studio-recital hall.

A new concept required:
All-purpose theatre

The large hall in either case should not be constructed as a conventional theatre with a solid proscenium frame, back of which a concert set is to be erected for orchestral concerts, as is the practice now. Where separate buildings cannot be constructed for each of the performing arts, as in New York and Washington, the all-purpose community theatre should be designed in accordance with the new concept of a flexible *Theatre-Concert Hall.* This new design will satisfy the needs of all the performing arts, including opera.

We have seen that the European opera theatres have evolved from traditions and premises quite different from those of the United States. On the other hand, we found in America the important germ cells of new, progressive ideas which go far beyond European traditions and encourage new approaches to theatrical architecture reflecting American conditions. Beautiful as many of the old European opera houses may be, they are precious relics of a world which has little to do with present-day America. Even in Europe, as we have seen, the traditional form of the opera house was retained only where it was a case of partial reconstruction after the war, as in Vienna or Berlin. Entirely new projects like the theatres in Bochum or Cologne do aim at developing new approaches, but the concept and production methods of opera in Europe remain basically bound by European traditions.

The American community requires a theatre hall able to accommodate all the performing arts and usable for many other purposes as well. The opera, ballet and drama repertories contain a majority of works which were conceived within the traditional proscenium. On the other hand, there are Greek, Shakespearean and modern plays best produced with the audience surrounding three sides of the action area. Again, the rapidly-growing number of arena-type theatres in the United States has made popular another type of production with the audience forming a circle around the action. Concert performances have still other exigencies. Telecasting from live theatre productions requires camera positioning on three sides and other technical conditions which we shall discuss later in the chapter on "Opera on Television." All these demands must be considered in the design of the theatre. And finally, the fact that the average American theatre must house productions drawing audiences of various sizes, ranging

180

from a famous guest Grand Opera company to a smaller local student performance, makes it advisable to create a flexible auditorium which can be adjusted to the size of the audience.

Obviously, if the various styles and production requirements of the performing arts are to be satisfied in one theatre, it must have a flexibility quite unimaginable in the European theatre of former times. Under the stimulus of conditions which prevail in the United States, the ingenuity of American theatre architects and technicians of today has made possible such a theatre.

Indigenous stage technique

As far as technical equipment for the new theatre is concerned, there is a great temptation to imitate the new, splendidly-equipped Middle-European opera houses. Here again, I would like to put in a word of warning. Different conditions of sponsorship and operation in America make it necessary to devise a correspondingly new approach to stage technique. If this is done, operatic production will neither lag behind Europe, as it often does today, nor imitate Europe in a prosaic manner. America can adopt the best in European stage technique, using it imaginatively and creatively to develop new, indigenous solutions. Thus, for the American stage director, the way will open to new and even more exciting possibilities of operatic production.

In general, the American theatre will require a less complicated technical system than is in use in Europe, particularly in Germany. The American theatre, in contrast to the European, will have to accommodate not only new productions of widely different types, but also guest productions of various kinds put on by outside groups. Its equipment must be able to satisfy a variety of demands. Facilities for the mounting, striking and removal of scenery, as well as the lighting system, must be simple in operation. Above all, the theatre cannot afford the great number of stagehands and electricians which are permanently employed by the European theatres. Therefore, stage equipment in our Civic Arts Center, like its architecture, should not be rigid and complicated but flexible, dependable and easy to operate.

American specialists available

We have already seen that American architects are bristling with new ideas about this type of flexible theatre form. American stage technicians and lighting specialists, consultants on acoustics and seating, experts in electronic sound control and television, are ready to apply their ideas to civic theatre building. We have noted that the foundations, too, are encouraging new architectural

181

projects, and that ANTA has set up an advisory agency for civic groups in need of expert information.

Two of my own sample patterns, illustrated here, show two basic design ideas for the construction of the new American theatre. These emphasize flexibility for multiple use.

Pattern I demonstrates the principle of one theatre accommodating both Grand Opera and *opéra comique* types of production (as well as medium-size productions). *Pattern II* illustrates the principle of maximum flexibility in an all-purpose theatre-concert hall.*

Pattern I:
Flexible Opera Theatre

Pattern I was made to demonstrate a program I submitted for the proposed Opera House at the National Cultural Center in Washington.** This project epitomizes the American problem: The Washington Opera House will have to accommodate guest productions of Grand Opera, as performed by the Metropolitan, for example, and productions of visiting opera and ballet companies. At the same time it must be suitable for operatic performances on a smaller scale, put on by companies like those of the New York City Center, as well as original productions by the local Opera Society. Therefore, the auditorium must have a maximum capacity of more than 3,000 seats, but at the same time it should have a flexibility adapting it to a more intimate type of production.

The stage must have the technical facilities to present opera and ballet in the traditional manner, with painted scenery consisting of wings, borders and backdrops. Consequently the gridiron system is required. It must also be able to handle productions in modern format using three-dimensional scenery and projections. Furthermore, keeping in mind the representative and nation-wide function of the National Cultural Center and the development of both commercial and educational television, the Washington Opera House should provide proper technical facilities for TV transmission from actual performances. Such facilities do not now exist in any opera house in the world.

To achieve this wide-ranging flexibility, I proposed the following ideas:

* The plans shown here have been conceived by this author and designed by Prof. Walther Unruh of Berlin, who is Technical Advisor for the Arts Centers in New York and Washington. Several of these technical ideas are new and are protected by U.S. Copyright.

** I presented this as a member of the Advisory Committee to the National Cultural Center in Washington. The other members of this Committee are Donald Oenslager, Ben Schlanger and Walther Unruh.

A new flexibility in the proscenium and orchestra area which will permit great variability to accommodate the two extreme types of production which are here called "Grand Opera Production," and "Opéra comique," or "Modern Opera Production."

Grand Opera Production, including operas like *Aida*, *Lohengrin*, etc. requires the classic proscenium, a view of the full depth of the stage, and the widest possible stage opening. Furthermore, the pit must accommodate a large orchestra, and the auditorium a maximum audience.

Opéra comique and Modern Opera Production, represented by operas like *Così fan tutte*, *The Barber of Seville* or Menotti's *The Consul*, require a closer contact between singing actor and audience. As in eighteenth century opera, the action frequently moves through the picture frame of the proscenium into the forestage area. This type of production needs less depth in the stage picture and often a smaller proscenium opening. Also, it is most effective in a smaller auditorium.

In order to present these two extreme types of production, as well as any intermediate type, the proscenium frame and orchestra area must have much greater adaptability than has hitherto been the case. The plan for such a theatre should include:

1. Flexibility in the orchestra zone so that it can be used in whole or in part as the action area, through a system of elevators that can raise individual sections to any height up to stage level as required (A).

2. Extension of the grid over the orchestra zone (B).

3. Placement of the iron or asbestos curtain in front of the regular orchestra pit (E).

4. Flexibility of the proscenium in both width and height: it should operate somewhat like a camera lens (C). As far as alteration of the width is concerned, I refer to the *Lamellen* system used in the Salzburg Festival House, which was opened in the summer of 1960. This system, which permits the modification of the proscenium from a width of approximately 48 to 100 feet, was suggested by me and Prof. Unruh.

5. The possibility of creating a second orchestra pit in front of the asbestos curtain, by mounting this area of the orchestra floor on elevators (G). The first rows of seats resting on this floor would then be removed, and the floor lowered to form the orchestra pit. This arrangement would suit intimate productions which do not require the full capacity of the auditorium.

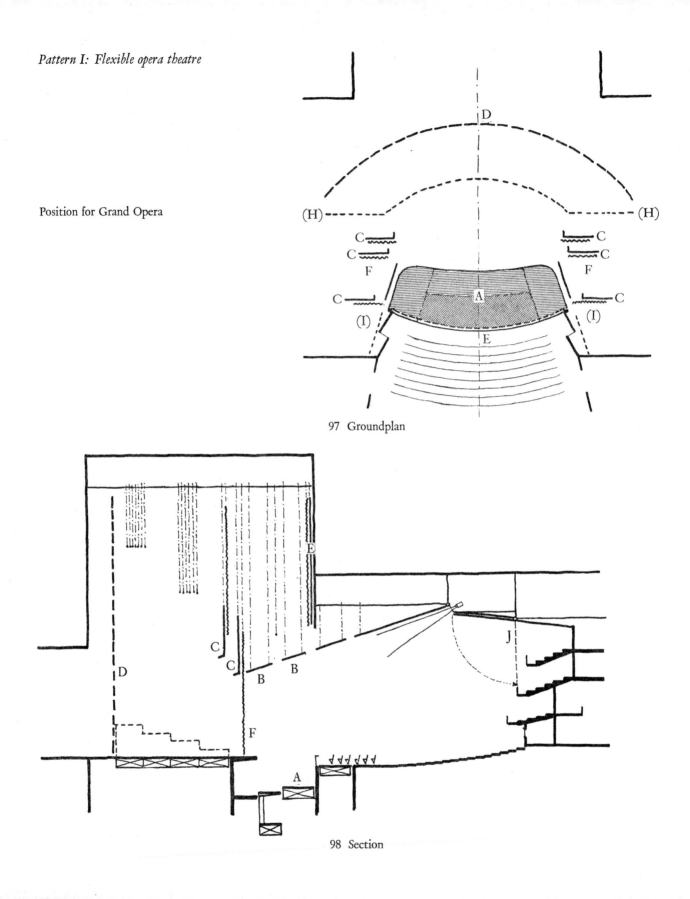

Pattern I: Flexible opera theatre

Position for Grand Opera

97 Groundplan

98 Section

Position for Opéra comique

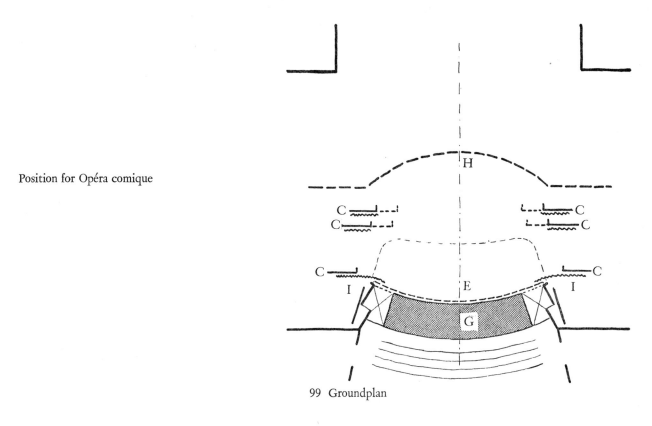

99 Groundplan

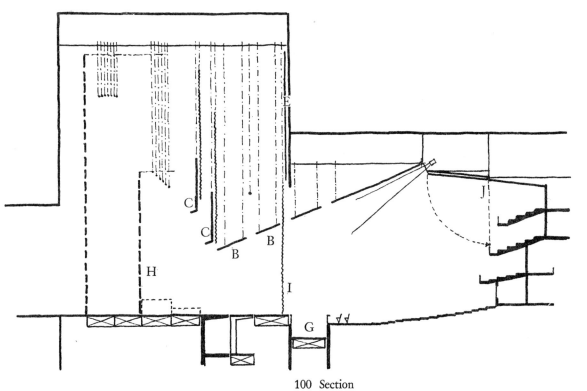

100 Section

6. A panel arrangement to shut off the balconies for smaller productions. These movable panels are to be designed in such a way as to satisfy the new acoustical requirements arising when they are employed (J).

7. A new solution for the placement of television cameras, which I will outline later.

The drawings illustrating Pattern I explain how these ideas work. They are not drawn to scale, but serve merely to present the basic ideas.

Designs 97 and 98 illustrate the "Position for Grand Opera" (*Groundplan* and *Section*):

1. The traditional orchestra pit is employed in the usual manner. The entire pit area is used, with additional players placed under the stage overhang (A).

2. The grid zone above the orchestra is closed off by shutters (B).

3. The proscenium is opened to its widest position (C).

4. Scenery can be set from the proscenium line to the maximum depth of the stage, if required for spectacular productions such as the Triumphal Scene of *Aida* (D).

5. The entire auditorium is in use, including the balconies (J).

Designs 99 and 100—"Position for Opéra comique" (*Groundplan* and *Section*):

1. The first rows of seats have been removed, and the floor lowered on elevators to form a new orchestra area for a smaller orchestra (G). Two small side stages are created in front of the asbestos curtain.

2. The full stage area between the proscenium and the asbestos curtain is used for action and scenery. Overhead shutters are opened, and the grid above the forestage zone is employed (B).

3. The proscenium is adjusted to a smaller opening (C).

4. The depth of the stage behind the proscenium is used only to a limited extent. A second cyclorama backs the stage picture (H).

5. The balconies are shut off by panels (J). The stage has been moved toward the audience. In planning sightlines for this arrangement it is necessary to consider only the boxes and the seats on the orchestra floor.

Pattern II:
Flexible Opera-Concert Hall

Pattern II was developed for the Curtis Institute of Music in Philadelphia. It illustrates the principle of flexibility in a hall suitable for both opera and concerts.

186

Plans 101–107 demonstrate the versatility of this theatre. Plan 101 shows the layout of the entire project, with the broken lines on the stage indicating the walls which form the concert set. In this case, the remainder of the stage remains hidden from the audience. Plan 102 shows the theatre as used for opera performances in the traditional style, employing the proscenium. Plan 103 retains the proscenium frame, with a flanking apron stage. This set-up would be used for plays or lecture-concerts. A projection screen is provided for lecture illustrations or television. Plan 104 demonstrates the use of the full stage with the proscenium moved out of sight. This form serves presentations of Greek or Shakespearean plays. Plan 105 shows the auditorium arranged as an arena theatre. The broken line indicates the wall which closes the auditorium in this case.

The house incorporates movable tormentors (illustrated in Plans 106 and 107). These tormentors can be placed in a free manner, in such positions as are indicated by the letters *A*, *B*, *C* and *D* in Plan 106. The flexibility of the tormentors at the sides is supplemented by the movable upper part of the proscenium and ceiling.

Other production requirements The American community theatre must have proper facilities for television transmission; and we must also take into consideration opera workshop and other educational performances. For these it would be very desirable to have, in addition to the theatre-concert hall, a small experimental studio theatre. This theatre, designed with similar adaptability, could also be used as a chamber music and recital hall. It should be connected with the bigger theatre to facilitate intercommunication, the shifting of scenery, costumes, etc. The studio theatre could also be used for rehearsals.

In every American community conditions of sponsorship, programming and production will vary. Consequently, the requirements of each Arts Center regarding the number of buildings, their size and equipment, will be different. But common to all American community theatres, except in the few large cities that can afford separate buildings for the individual arts, will be the abandonment of the rigid scheme of the European box-proscenium opera theatre in favor of a flexibility satisfying the requirements of all the performing arts. Only this new concept can supply a realistic solution to the problems presented by conditions in the United States, and only this type of theatre will enable opera to integrate itself with the other arts within the American community.

Pattern II: Flexible opera-concert hall

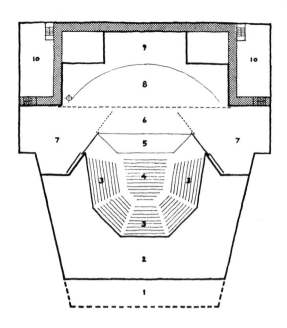

1 ENTRANCE HALL   6/8 MAIN STAGE
2 LOBBY   7 SIDE STAGE
3 AUDITORIUM AMPHITHEATRE   9 BACK STAGE
4 AUDITORIUM PARTERRE   10 DRESSING ROOMS
5 ORCHESTRA - PIT   A.S.O.

101 General lay-out and use for concerts

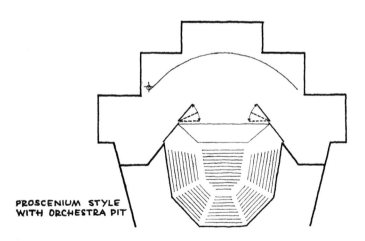

PROSCENIUM STYLE
WITH ORCHESTRA PIT

102 Arrangement for opera performances with proscenium

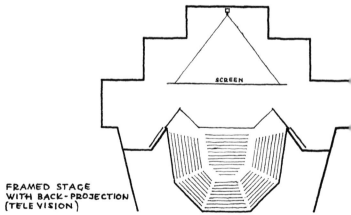

FRAMED STAGE
WITH BACK-PROJECTION
(TELEVISION)

SCREEN

103 For plays with proscenium, or lecture-recital

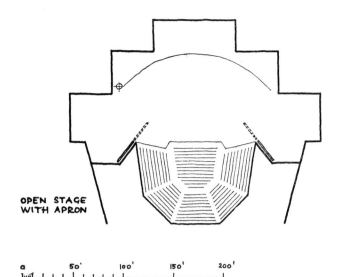

OPEN STAGE
WITH APRON

0   50'   100'   150'   200'

104 Arrangement for Greek or Shakespearean plays

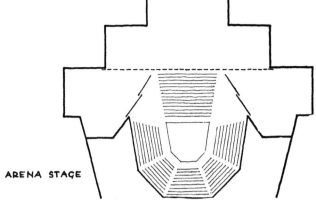

ARENA STAGE

105 As arena theatre

Movable tormentors

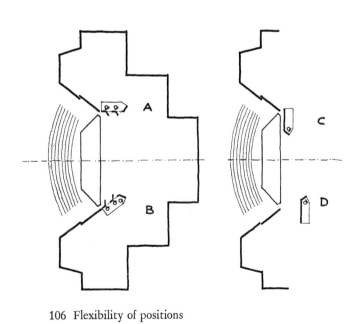

A

B

C

D

106 Flexibility of positions

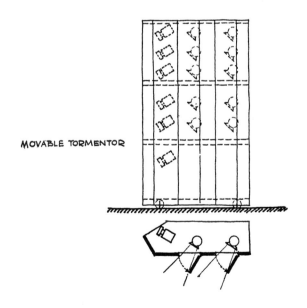

MOVABLE TORMENTOR

107 Plan and section

3. ARTISTIC POLICY

Our survey of the artistic policies which have guided operatic production in Europe and America leads to the conclusion that traditional European systems cannot be applied to opera production in America without decisive modification. In most American cities there are at present neither the audiences nor the financial means that are available in Europe.

Opera in our time

Moreover, it is questionable whether these traditional approaches are still workable today. When Gustav Mahler espoused the repertory system with great success in Vienna, and Toscanini followed the *stagione* system in Milan, while Gatti-Casazza employed features of both systems in New York, modern transportation and communication systems did not exist. Today Vienna and Munich, Milan and Rome, are mere hours away from New York and Boston. As a result the day is past when any opera house can write exclusive contracts with a group of world-famous artists and look upon them as private property. Even the smaller American cities now demand the outstanding artists whom they know from Metropolitan broadcasts or from recordings, and the airplane makes this artistic exchange possible.

Since the public insists on "stars," and the managements bow to these requests for obvious, though not always entirely valid reasons, it is no longer possible to keep an artistic ensemble intact for any length of time. Any attempt to engage a leading artist for the necessary rehearsal period plus repeat performances over a matter of weeks or months, as required by the present subscription systems, must fail. We have seen the consequence—the breakup of the opera ensemble— not only in America but also in Europe.

On the other hand, television has made it possible for more people to see and hear a single performance of an opera than were able to witness the same opera in all the performances given by a major opera house during the past fifty years. Touring companies once gave people in distant cities their only chance to see a first-rate opera performance. But touring has become very expensive, and for this reason several companies have ended their touring activities in recent years. This loss has been partly balanced by television. Over the long period of development from European court subsidy to American democratic sponsorship, from candlelight to electricity, from stage coach to jet travel, the costs and conditions of production have undergone changes which must obviously be reflected, eventually, in artistic and managerial policy.

The logical thing to do, in my opinion, is to approach this problem head-on and find a solution tailored to the facts as they exist. The old systems amortized the cost of an opera production through repeat performances—as many as possible over months and years. I would advocate a new system of *rapid* amortization through development of an operatic "package" production. Each production would be conceived and carried out to serve two or even three purposes, namely:

(*a*) Live performance in the opera house.

(*b*) Television transmission from the performance in the opera house (or live studio telecast using the entire original theatre production).

(*c*) Videotaping or filming.

This approach would be very practical at the present time in America, where it is not yet possible for most communities to plan an extended opera season, and where integration of opera into the existing symphony concert series seems the most expedient way to achieve opera production. In the present concert system one program is repeated one to three times. In place of a concert performance of opera, a staged operatic production could be given two or three performances as part of the regular symphony subscription series, as previously outlined. The last, or an additional, performance could be put on for education purposes and transmitted by television and, possibly, videotaped for educational television. Let us put aside for the moment the technical questions involved, which I will discuss in "Opera on Television," and restate clearly the new principle: replacement of the old repertory and *stagione* systems, in which an opera production was amortized by repeat performances over months and years, by a new system under which a few live performances of a production in the opera house, followed by a transmission on TV, videotape or film could be expected to defray a great part, if not all, of the production costs.

This method will have many advantages:

First, it will keep the operatic ensemble intact for the relatively short period of actual rehearsals and performances.

Second, it will, for everyone concerned, make it possible to defray the effort and expense of a highly artistic production based on a sufficient budget.

Third, it will make opera available to a much larger audience.

Fourth, it will integrate opera into the present concert subscription system of the symphony orchestra without substantial changes in that system, at least during the present stage of development.

Co-operation with the other arts I believe the best solution to opera production for most American cities lies in integration of opera and symphony. In situations where the symphony society undertakes opera production, it should be possible to expand the program from two or three operas produced during one season to two or three short opera seasons during the year, scheduled before and after the concert season, and possibly in mid-season. Where an established opera company already exists, collaboration might be limited to regular employment of the symphony orchestra by the opera company. In cities like New York, the Philharmonic and the Metropolitan Opera Orchestra are fully occupied with their own separate activities. In smaller American cities, however, I maintain that the best solution will be found in complete integration of the two activities, as in Middle-European cities. There would be, however, this difference: the former operatic system of repeat performances would be replaced by the "package" system proposed above.

The performing arts program should not be limited to symphony concerts and opera productions, however. The program should include light opera and dance as well. This seems only natural since these arts use the same elements. Close collaboration with drama and fine arts groups is also important.

Co-operation of all these groups will guarantee the extension of the artistic season into what will amount to a year-round operation. A festival in the late spring or summer, which might include symphony concerts, opera, light opera and musical comedy, dance performances, "pop" concerts, jazz programs and fine arts exhibitions, would not only bring welcome relaxation to the citizens but would also provide financial security for the artistic personnel. Such security is distressingly lacking in America today.

Repertory modernized The repertory of the American opera company should not be limited to the popular standard works, but should also include contemporary works and old operas which are rarely performed. The success of Menotti's operas, and the popular acclaim which greeted the last spring seasons of the New York City Center Opera Company during which new American operas were performed,

192

are proof of the public interest in operas outside the bread-and-butter repertory. The operatic repertory cannot stop with *Rosenkavalier* and *Turandot* any more than the legitimate theatre could restrict itself to works written more than thirty-five years ago. The popularity of American opera workshops, which perform a majority of modern operas, is further proof of the interest in new works.

Again: Opera in English? The question of performing opera in English is, as we mentioned before, not so much an artistic problem as it is a simple question of communication between opera and audience. If opera is to reach the people, it will have to speak the language of the people. One might flirt with a lady who is beautiful for a little while without understanding her language, but it is not possible to think of a permanent relationship on that superficial basis. If community opera accepts the principle of singing opera in the vernacular, that does not dogmatically exclude occasional performances of opera in the original language, particularly by guest opera companies and extraordinary singers, or at festivals and for educational purposes. It makes no sense, however, for American or foreign artists to sing opera in bad Italian or German or French or Russian for an audience which does not understand any of these languages, under the pretext of "art." Of course, singing in English, like singing in any other language, requires proper study and coaching in musical enunciation. The problem would be made immeasurably more simple if good translations could be commissioned by music publishers and an agreement reached between leading opera companies and publishers, establishing certain translations as standard.

Importance of light opera The performance of classic operettas and the best Broadway musicals by the American opera company will not only prove to be good business, but will also help educate the audience and the young singers. The lighter sister of opera will help guide the uninitiated public to more serious works, while giving inexperienced performers an opportunity to learn how to move naturally on stage.

A working relationship between opera companies and opera schools and workshops is of great importance, because the future of opera will depend on our finding and assisting young artists. After they have completed their basic studies, the best place for them to get their final training is in the theatre, where as apprentices they can learn by watching accomplished performing artists. This will also be of help to the opera company in another way. The young artists could understudy all the roles and be called upon to sing them in case of illness of the leading singers. This is the best investment an opera theatre can make—to give talented young artists an opportunity to gain experience. They will learn through actual performance and by making mistakes. I will never forget the words of Bruno Walter, when he invited me to work with him as stage director at the Florence May Festival in 1935. "I have heard so many terrible things you did," he said, "that I thought there must be some talent." And he entrusted me with a production which was the beginning of my career in the international field.

Stars that do not shine

The manager of an American opera company should not overestimate the so-called "name" singer. While there are a few stars who really draw big audiences because of their personality and voice, there are many more who only think they do. On many occasions, one guest artist who alone could provide the necessary box-office "draw" is backed up by three other singers from New York who are prohibitively expensive and take work away from deserving local or regional talent. The manager, therefore, will do well to reach a proper balance between "name" artists, if these are essential for box-office reasons—and if they agree to take part in the necessary number of rehearsals—and the many excellent young artists who are available in America, a number of them probably

Local resources and public relations

located in his own neighborhood. The same considerations hold for the employment of the local chorus and members of the local dance school. Close collaboration with local forces will not only strengthen the artistic development of these organizations, but also lead to good public relations between the opera company and the community.

As far as the scenic end of the production is concerned, the same policy should be followed. Normally stage director and designer should not be imported, nor scenery and costumes made or rented outside the community, unless this will actually result in a higher quality of performance than could be achieved by using local resources. More often than not there are talented young artists available in the local community or nearby, in music or drama groups or schools. What they lack in experience is often compensated for by the fact that they can devote more time to the preparation of the production than guest artists who arrive on the scene to stay only a few days. In other cases, it might be advisable to engage local directors for the season as assistants to accomplished professional guests, or to send them to study or work in major opera houses at home or abroad, so that they can get the necessary experience for the work in their own community.

Staging dictated by the music Regarding staging, I would advocate simplicity, not only for financial reasons, but also for artistic ones. Opera direction is not to be confused with play or film direction. A play director may be able to achieve good acting, but if the acting does not reinforce and reflect the demands of the music, it will not be good opera direction. In masterworks, at least, the music is always paramount. The same thing is true of the scenery; it must be designed with the requirements of the music in mind. Much of the musical expression in opera is concentrated in arias, ensembles, pauses or interludes. These cannot be handled with an eye to action.

For these reasons, opera requires stage directors who are musical. This does not mean, however, that a drama director with musical understanding could not adapt himself to the laws of opera. In fact such a man, if he is willing to learn the particular operatic styles by working in collaboration with an opera conductor who understands the problems of the stage, may well turn out to be the best choice for the local opera company, since there are as yet very few professional opera directors available.

As we have said, opera makes special demands of its own with regard to the style and form of the scenery. The scenery must permit the proper distribution, relationship and movement of soloists, chorus voices and supers in accordance with musical indications. The same is true for the lighting and its timing. Collaboration with a musical stage director and conductor can help the designer

Collaboration with other fine arts desirable decisively. In choosing a designer, it might be advisable not to seek always for theatrical professionals, but to see what the fine arts group of the community has to offer. A talented painter or architect might bring to the production a new artistic quality of form and color that will lift it out of the ordinary routine. Of course, designers inexperienced with opera should not be used in the case of operas which are difficult from a stage-technical point of view. Modern opera production, however, should rely more on stimulating the imagination of the listener than on limiting it by realistic description.

In the words of Robert Edmond Jones, who was equally great, whether designing for the legitimate theatre or for opera, "A good scene should be not a picture, but an image." Opera production must help the audience create its own world when listening to the music. Therefore it will require, in the first place, simplicity and careful designing of space and costumes, imaginative use of color, appropriate and carefully-timed lighting; and last, but not least, concentration on the singing actor.

Opera—the world of imagination

Good opera direction is at the opposite pole from Hollywood realism. Opera is a different kind of theatre. To quote Robert Edmond Jones again—and his words apply to the great opera theatre of the past and predict the opera theatre of tomorrow—"The realistic theatre, we may remember, is less than a hundred years old. But the theatre—great theatre, world theatre—is far older than that, so many centuries older that by comparison it makes our little candid-camera theatre seem like something that was thought up only the day before yesterday. We need not be impatient. A brilliant fresh theatre will presently appear."*

4. OPERA SCHOOL

Nowhere in the world today is there a larger and more promising group of young operatic artists than America possesses. Nowhere are there better music schools or more opportunities for training, particularly in opera workshops connected with universities. And nowhere is more being done to assist the training of young artists, through scholarships from private individuals, foundations and government sources. Yet nowhere in the world is there *less* opportunity for the student, once he has completed his training, to apply it. It is self-evident that American opera companies should take advantage of this wealth of fine operatic material. These young American singers have not only good voices, but also convincing physical appearance, acting ability, musicianship and the willingness to study and rehearse.

Confusion of aims and standards

The operatic training picture in America today is very confused. Among the thousands of ambitious aspirants there are many who begin their studies in out-of-the-way places where operatic standards have not been established, and where

* Robert Edmond Jones, *The Dramatic Imagination* (New York: Theatre Arts Books, 1941).

there are frequently no teachers to develop talent on a professional level. Even opera workshops, tied into a university curriculum, cannot concentrate on achieving professional standards of voice training and musicianship but must consider the academic requirements of general higher education. Yet American opera singers develop despite every handicap, in a confused world that mixes professionalism and dilettantism, academic standards and inadequate craftsmanship, idealism and commercialism and even graft.

These young singers, trained or untrained, must compete for a pitifully small number of positions in professional opera companies. At the same time they must meet the high professional standards set by leading artists, because the audience expects it of them.

It is therefore imperative that the present confusion in training for opera be ended. What is required is a distinct professional definition of the aims. This definition should arrive at a clear separation of objectives and training programs as these relate to: (*a*) the music school or conservatory of music; (*b*) the workshop; and (*c*) the professional opera company.

Curriculum for the music school   The *music school* or *conservatory* should provide purely practical instruction in music for professional purposes. In the field of opera, the curriculum should comprise voice training, solfège, piano, language instruction, English enunciation and speech, acting for the stage and for television, body-training and dance, fencing, costuming and make-up and history of music and the theatre.

There can be no doubt that, with all due respect to the study of acting and general musicianship, the training of the voice must claim the singer's major attention. Careful and unhurried study of the *bel canto* method is the foundation of the singing artist's career. The process of vocal development must not be hurried, since the vocal cords develop in a physical process which cannot be speeded up artificially. Unfortunately, the need to earn a living often interrupts the development of talented singers. Many promising voices have disappeared from the scene after a short career, due to a forced schedule of vocal training and the tackling of operatic parts for which these voices were not ready.

While it is true that classical vocal training is facilitated by the pure vowels of the Italian language, the widely-held opinion that singing in English is "not good for the voice" cannot be accepted, any more than it can be maintained that it hurts the voice to sing German. Lotte Lehmann, Flagstad, Schwarzkopf and Fischer-Dieskau are by no means inferior to Italians in the art of singing; and Warren, Peerce, Tucker, Farrell and many other Americans have given ample proof that a good singer sings well in any language.

Another question, however, is the matter of training in English enunciation, which is lacking in many schools. It would be advisable to give at least as much attention to diction in English as is devoted to Italian, French and German.

Dramatic training is enormously useful to the young singers, as long as it is taught with the demands of opera in mind. Acting in opera must reflect the musical score. Knowledge of the particular characteristics of operatic style as opposed to the style of spoken drama is, of course, of the greatest importance for the operatic composer and librettist as well as the stage director and designer. These artists require for their preparation a curriculum of courses at the conservatory, combined with additional study at the university's drama and fine arts schools and at its opera workshop.

Program for the opera workshop

In contrast with the practical music instruction given by the music schools and conservatories, or by private teachers in place of it, there is the experimental study provided by the *opera workshops*, particularly those of colleges and universities. Opera workshops should present operatic studies, in general, on the academic level and should give experience in performance on an experimental basis. They should therefore be open to any student whose higher education includes the study of opera, as well as to the student heading for a professional career as an operatic artist who wants both to enlarge his general knowledge of opera and gain practical experience by participating in performances. The opera workshop is of particular value to composers, librettists, scenic designers and directors who want to study various styles of opera production and experiment with new works written for and performed by the workshop. It is also important for future teachers, music critics and the public at large, by providing a deeper understanding of opera.

Professional opera company

The third institution, the *professional opera company*, requires the services of accomplished artists who have been trained in the music school and composers and directors who have developed new ideas in the opera workshop.

Unfortunately, a clear definition of purpose between the different functions of these three institutions is, to the detriment of the student, frequently lacking today.

Music schools should, first of all, perform standard operas in training their students: the works of Bellini and Rossini, for example, for the study of Italian opera; Mozart and Weber for German opera; and Berlioz or Massenet for French opera. Most music school performances should be presented in the original languages. Instead, many music schools today concentrate on presenting modern operas in English. University opera workshops, which ought to be devoting their efforts to experimental productions for study purposes, often try to stage standard operas on a professional level. And professional opera companies, which might well include established modern works as part of their repertory, rely mostly on the operas of the past. The student is given difficult modern roles at the music school, where he should be trying to settle his vocal problems and to acquire the standard repertory, while the opera workshop frequently presents him to the public in standard roles often performed with insufficient preparation due to the other demands of the academic curriculum.

Without intending in any sense to minimize the great contribution of the American opera workshop—it is often the only place where the young operatic artist can try his wings on a stage—I nevertheless believe that a fourth institution should be added to these three in order to bridge the gap between the elementary practical instruction of the music school and the professional requirements of the opera company. This new institution should be a *Master Class* or *Center for Advanced Operatic Performance*, to be administered by the music school. It should offer advanced study for the school's own students, as well as for students from other schools, provided they are admitted on the basis of high professional qualification. The master class should include composers, conductors, stage directors, choreographers and designers, and should have at its disposal facilities for full operatic performance.

This master class, or studio theatre, should operate like a professional organization and achieve professional standards of production. It should have a close working relationship with both the music school and the professional opera company. Qualified directors and singers of the opera company should be engaged as instructors. Outstanding figures in local drama and fine arts groups should be engaged to train scenic designers. The working relationship between the studio theatre of the music school and the opera company should be very close, while the relationship between the university workshop and the professional opera company should be limited to the extent that the opera workshop would serve as an experimental showcase for trying out new operas, conductors, directors and designers, and provide a forum for the discussion of new works, in all of which the opera company would take an interest.

Active relationship between opera theatre and school

The studio theatre, however, would re-establish the tradition referred to by Richard Wagner; namely, the tradition of an organic relationship between the great opera theatre and the music school. During the Eighteenth Century in Naples and Paris the famous opera theatres and the equally famous conservatories worked together. It was the task of the conservatories to "conserve" and teach the national styles which had been developed in the great theatres through personal contact between the students and the leading artists. In a similar way, professional American opera companies and music schools can achieve the best possible training of the young artist. The student, who would live and work in close contact with the performing artists, would not only be admitted to rehearsals and performances of the opera company, but would also be requested to understudy the roles of the leading artists. In case of illness, the student would be called upon to sing the rehearsal or performance. This would be the best way for him to gain practical experience, and it could possibly lead to regular employment with the company. It would provide the young artist with the same practical apprenticeship, under a highly qualified professional, which the young painter, doctor or engineer practices before he attempts to establish himself on his own. Thus the music school will not stand aside from the opera company in academic isolation but will play a constructive part in the performing program of the community opera company and benefit from its professional standards.

5. OPERA ON TELEVISION

Only one more element is needed to complete our program for organizing the American opera of the future—television. As it seemed logical to seek the collaboration of the other performing and fine arts that can contribute to operatic production, it is imperative to include the newest medium in the family of performing techniques. For television has demonstrated from the start its interest in opera and proved to be of great value to this art.

200

Collaboration between local opera organizations and television companies not only opens up new possibilities for the distribution of opera throughout the entire American community, but holds far-reaching artistic, technical, organizational and financial implications for the future of American community opera itself. We have already mentioned three forms of operatic telecasting: (*a*) studio performance, (*b*) transmission of opera from actual theatre performances, and (*c*) videotaping or filming of opera, particularly when productions are designed with television in mind.

Studio telecast

This is, at the moment, the only form of TV transmission of opera being used in America. In Chapter 5, Part II, we discussed the artistic and technical features of the productions currently being transmitted. These achieve a great deal of dramatic realism in the presentation of opera. Aside from technical concern with proper camera positioning and special lighting designed specifically for TV transmission, emphasis has been placed on convincing physical appearance of the young singer, good acting, clear enunciation in the language of the audience, and visibility of details of the operatic play. These are virtues which opera house performances too often lack.

But the striving to achieve visual reality in studio production also involves serious risk of distorting opera. Since the television audience is to a great extent identical with the movie audience, and since television production techniques resemble film techniques, the operatic television producer is frequently tempted to utilize a style of scenic interpretation and acting which is in conflict with the essential character of opera itself. While good opera is obviously "theatre," it is a special kind of theatre. It is definitely *musical* theatre. If this is forgotten, the production, as opera, suffers.

The close-up eye of the television camera can immeasurably enhance the sense of audience participation in opera. For instance, in the first act of *La Bohème*, the public, with Rodolfo, can visually caress Mimi's freezing little hand; and the audience, through the camera, can witness in close-up the growing adoration in the eyes of the two young lovers. But the technical possibilities of studio television frequently conflict with the artistic premises of opera. The standstills of action at musical high points, the emotional symbolism, the spaciousness of

201

the chorus scenes, all create problems for the television director. It is, therefore, not surprising that the best operatic studio productions have been of intimate or realistic works; and, in particular, of modern operas either written for or adapted for television, such as Menotti's *Amahl and the Night Visitors*, Britten's *Billy Budd* or Prokofieff's *War and Peace*. Grand Opera of the *Aida* or *Lohengrin* type has been understandably omitted.

But while television opera must remain opera, it must also remain television. It is not surprising that the television director, dazzled by the fairy gifts from movieland, should frequently approach opera as though he were producing a film. But obviously making a film is quite a different aesthetic and technical problem from producing a live TV performance. The greatest asset of television is its ability to transmit an actual event *while it is happening*. Applied to opera, this brings up the second form of operatic telecasting: transmission from actual theatre performances.

Theatre television

The Cinderella of operatic TV transmission

Although direct transmission of opera from the actual theatre performance is today the stepchild among methods of operatic transmission, I have no doubt that because of its unique advantages it will rise successfully to a glamorous new life as soon as the technical requirements for this type of telecast are satisfied. I can see my director colleagues in television shaking their heads over this statement, but it is made with conviction based on my own practical experience in American, Italian and Austrian television.

Up to the present, theatre television has suffered from lack of proper technical preparation. Three facts must be considered: (*a*) Theatre transmissions, so far, have been made only of productions that were originally designed without any regard for the requirements of telecasting; (*b*) except for the few productions previously noted, telecasts have usually been made without the necessary technical preparations; and (*c*) the architectural layout of conventional theatres from which operas have been telecast does not permit proper transmission.

The traditional use of the proscenium frame has resulted in a technique of operatic production which stresses a frontal, two-dimensional picture view. This approach is quite the opposite of the in-the-round space concept of television, which looks at its objects from three or four sides. Moreover, the traditional operatic theatre production rarely emphasizes convincing physical appearance or good acting; the close-up camera eye is an unpitying observer of such weaknesses. In addition, the theatre production usually lacks the three-dimensional scenery and lighting required by television.

These obstacles to satisfactory telecasting from theatre productions can be overcome by the program outlined previously, which specifies a new type of theatre, and productions of opera conceived from the beginning to meet the requirements of theatre, telecast and film.

Problems not yet solved

Television production experts have not as yet solved many problems of "live" transmission of opera, even in studio productions. Where to put the orchestra, and how to maintain contact between conductor and singers are two questions which have received improvised and unsatisfactory answers. The problem is usually resolved in studio productions either by pre-recording the sound, or by moving the conductor and the orchestra into another studio away from the singers. Modern opera theatres have provided for TV cable connections, but as far as I know, no satisfactory provisions have been made for three-sided photography with cameras out of sight.

In addition to the suggestions I made previously for the new opera theatre, I propose herewith a new architectural solution for the handling of television cameras in theatres or arenas (see Plans 108–111).* The main feature of this plan is a "television floor" in the auditorium (K). This floor, which interrupts the ascending floor of the orchestra seating area, runs around the entire auditorium. It provides a large room and corridor, in which the cameras can move freely to view the production from any side. The cameras would be entirely hidden from the audience, unless people in the first rows of seats intentionally turned back to look at them. Furthermore, a retractable camera would be suspended from the ceiling of the auditorium. The conductor and orchestra would be positioned below the sightline of the cameras that face the stage straight on. The stage area is carried forward into the auditorium. With cameras moving freely around the auditorium and placed also on either side of the stage, television photography is secured from any point within a radius of 270 degrees around the zone of action.

* This idea is protected by United States Copyright.

Plan of a theatre for
television transmission of
operatic performances
(Copyrighted designs)

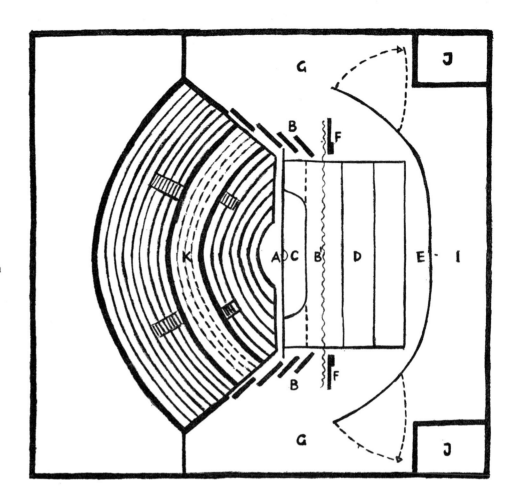

108 Groundplan

A Asbestos curtain
B Movable proscenium
B¹ Show curtain
C Orchestra pit
D Stage elevators
E Cyclorama
F Tormentors
G Side stages
H Workshops
I Backstage
J Storage
K Television floor
L Suspended TV camera
M Foyer
N Paint floor
O Driveway

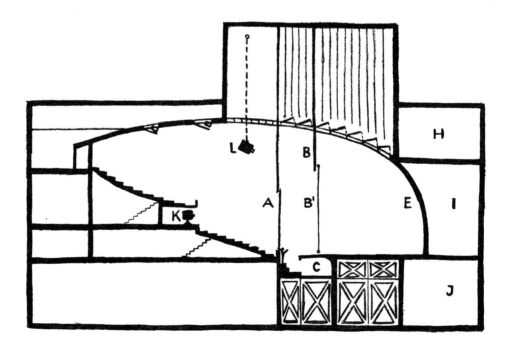

109 Section

Plan of an auditorium
usable for television
transmission of operatic
performances
(Copyrighted designs)

110 Groundplan

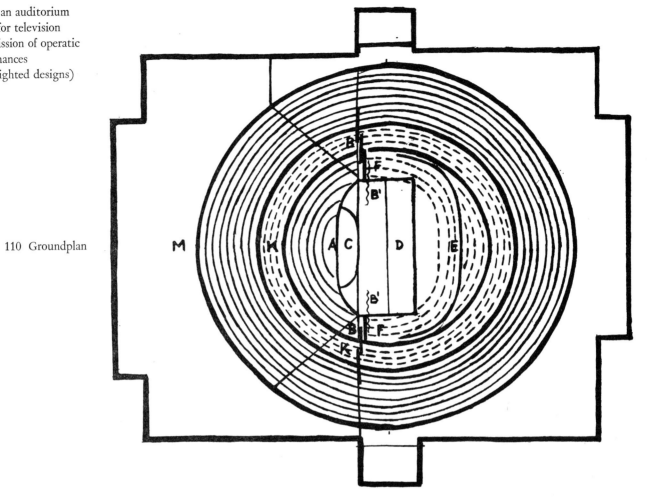

Explanation of signs
see page 204

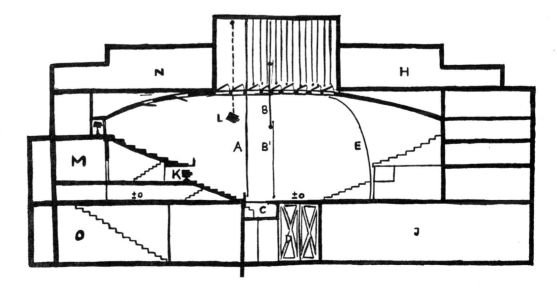

111 Section

Since the production to be televised would be conceived from the beginning with television transmission in mind, following the suggestions outlined in the chapter on "Artistic Policy," the casting of the singers, the language used, the scenery and the rehearsal conditions would be approximately the same as for a studio telecast. In addition, we would have the excitement and immediacy of a transmission during the actual performance of an opera in the theatre, with an audience present. To make certain that the telecast is technically perfect, I suggest that the transmission be made from a special performance at lower prices, possibly for schools. This would permit technicians to make all the light adjustments required by the television cameras, while still preserving the participation of an audience.

Opera and Film

Opera performance on film

If the new theatre, and productions conceived and carried out specifically with TV in mind, result in technically satisfactory television programs, it would be logical to take a further step: the same productions could easily be used for videotape recording or filming, possibly during the off-season months. Films made of such productions would not be Hollywood or Cine Città film versions of operas, but documentaries that could be considered the visual counterpart to recordings.

It seems obvious that collaboration between opera and television companies would be mutually beneficial in all three forms of operatic telecasting. The television company would gain prestige by using productions of the opera company, and when a studio production of opera was desired, the television company would have at its disposition the common pool of young artists, orchestra, translations, the entire musical preparation, the costumes and at least part of the scenery. Economically speaking, both organizations would profit from close association, since a technically outstanding theatre transmission should be a welcome proposition to commercial sponsors, and quite possibly bring returns from future pay television systems as well as the promised videotape machines for home use.

The opera company would benefit from collaboration with television, from artistic, economic and sociological points of view. Artistically, opera can learn from television how to achieve visual truth, good ensemble and convincing detail.

Television will also encourage use of the language the audience understands. Economically speaking, opera can gain substantial financial support from commercial sponsorship of operatic performances produced for multiple use in theatre, television and film performances. If income from commercial sources were added to sponsorship, the result might well be a balanced operatic budget. From the sociological viewpoint, the development of educational television in all its aspects opens up new horizons for opera, including theatre transmissions and the employment of videotape recording and films in classroom instruction. Television can bring opera to a vast new audience, which so far has had no real acquaintance with opera; and it is this new group that will finally establish opera as an art essential to the life of the American community.

American Opera—not a dream   We have come to the end of our survey of operatic production in Europe and the United States. Our proposed program for opera in America lies before you. I hear some voices saying, "Dreams!" I can only reply that the real fantasy is in thinking that opera can establish itself successfully in America in any other way. It must build solidly on the foundations already in existence, and take advantage of the forces presently at work in America. These foundations and these forces are not dreams—they are the only real facts. From these foundations opera in the United States will rise and find its proper place in American cultural life. In the end American opera will be not an unimaginative imitation of opera in Europe, but rather, as an integral part of American community life, it will become a new and even more exciting art form. The American opera of tomorrow will embody the dynamic, creative spirit of the American people in a cultural achievement recognized and honored not only in the United States but throughout the world.

Index

The numbers in italics refer to the illustrations

Index

The numbers in italics refer to the illustrations